Praise for
VISIBLE

Too often, talented professionals stay stuck in the shadows. *Visible* is a masterclass in stepping forward confidently—without selling out or burning out.
— **Dorie Clark**, executive education faculty at Columbia Business School and Wall Street Journal bestselling author of The Long Game

Visible is a smart, no-nonsense guide for anyone ready to step into a bigger role without selling their soul. It tackles the real challenge of leadership transitions: being seen as ready before you feel—or are—fully there. With sharp insight and practical tools, it helps you shift how you show up, how you're seen, and ultimately, who you believe yourself to be.
— **Professor Herminia Ibarra FBA**, Charles Handy Professor of Organisational Behaviour, London Business School

Irony alert! Working harder can make you easier to ignore. Here's the way to get seen.
— **Michael Bungay Stanier**, *The Coaching Habit*

In *Visible*, May Busch brings her life and her career experiences into one cohesive "how to" approach to achieving success in both. A model for presenting and promoting who you truly are.
— **Craig Weatherup**, former CEO of Pepsi-Cola

Visible shines a light on one of the most overlooked truths in leadership and career growth: hard work alone is not enough. With honesty, insight, and wisdom drawn from her own remarkable journey, May Busch shows professionals how to rise by showing

their talent and efforts — without losing themselves. Read it, apply it, and you'll discover how to step forward with confidence, earn the recognition you deserve, and lead with authenticity.
— **Dr. Marshall Goldsmith**, Thinkers50 #1 Executive Coach and New York Times bestselling author of *The Earned Life*, *Triggers*, and *What Got You Here Won't Get You There*

Most career books tell you to hustle harder, shout louder, or play politics. *Visible* shows you how to rise without betraying your values. Drawn from real scars and real wins, it gives you the tools to get seen, heard, and valued. If you're tired of being overlooked, this is the shift you've been waiting for.
— **Keith Ferrazzi**, #1 New York Times bestselling author and Founder, *Ferrazzi Greenlight*

As a university president, I have seen many capable graduates stall in their careers—not from lack of effort or talent, but from lack of visibility. In *Visible*, May Busch outlines how professionals can rise with integrity in today's competitive workplaces by not just doing great work, but by making that work visible to the right people. If this playbook were available to more of our graduates before they leave campus, they would advance more quickly during their careers. Smart, ethical, and empowering.
— **Michael M. Crow**, President, Arizona State University

In this beautiful new book, author May Busch provides a compassionate guide to career mastery. Drawing from her own firsthand business experiences, she explains the importance of visibility, people skills, and confidence—and gently guides readers on how to do great work and build career success. Her compelling stories will keep you turning the page.
— Amy C. Edmondson, Novartis Professor of Leadership, Harvard Business School; author of *Right Kind of Wrong: The Science of Failing Well*

VISIBLE
VISIBLE
VISIBLE
VISIBLE

How to Advance Your Career

Without Playing Politics, Selling Your Soul,

or Working Yourself into the Ground

MAY BUSCH

SUMMIT PRESS
Publishers

Printed in the United States of America
First Printing, 2025
ISBN: 979-8-9852063-8-8

Library of Congress Number: 2025915445

Summit Press Publishers
P.O. Box 1356
Intervale, New Hampshire 03845

For information about working with May Busch, visit www.maybusch.com.

For bulk sales, email us at author@summitpresspublishers.com.

To the Career Mastery community
and good people everywhere.

AUTHOR'S NOTE

This book began as an expansion of my first book, *Accelerate*, but evolved into something new. *Visible* approaches career advancement through a different lens—focusing on how to demonstrate your potential for the next level, rather than just excelling in your current role.

If you've read *Accelerate*, you'll recognize some core concepts presented here with fresh depth and new insights, alongside completely new strategies and tools. If this is your first encounter with my work, you can dive right in.

You'll also find additional resources to help implement these ideas at www.thevisiblebook.com/resources.

The stories throughout this book are real. Names have been changed to protect privacy, with two exceptions: Dick Fisher, former president of Morgan Stanley, and my friend Wendy—both of whom deserve recognition for being consummate rainmakers.

TABLE OF CONTENTS

INTRODUCTION

At first, I didn't see the resemblance. But the longer I chatted with the lawyer from Portugal, the more I felt as though I was talking to my younger self. I saw the same dedication and desire to do well, the same strong work ethic, the same willingness to redouble her efforts to deliver perfect results for her company ... and the same mistaken belief that her work should speak for itself.

She, too, had success in the early stages of her career. But then she continued to produce excellent results yet seemed to have hit a plateau. She hadn't seen a promotion or been offered a coveted project in over a year, even though she was working twice as hard as others. She felt overlooked, ignored.

More than once, she'd been told to "play the game": to suck up to the big boss; go out for drinks after work with the "in crowd"; watch football on the weekend to talk sports on Mondays; pontificate at meetings; and engage in nonstop self-promotion. But playing that game was the last thing she wanted to do. Like so many ambitious professionals, she wanted advancement without sacrificing her values or personal time.

Exhausted from work, worry, and next to no free time for herself, she feared burnout before she ever had the chance to achieve her ambitions. While she knew she was dealing with high-class problems, she was frustrated and unsure what she could do about them.

I looked around the room at the others who had attended my presentation. There were some two hundred people. No doubt many of them felt that same sense of stagnation in their careers. The approach that had gotten them this far—*keep your head down, do excellent work, and expect to get recognized and rewarded*—was no longer working. They wanted to get ahead, but not at any cost. That's why they were attending an event on authentic leadership. They were looking for the key to advance to the next level in their careers without selling their souls or burning out.

It was puzzling. Delivering excellent results had been enough to get them to this point. Now, however, it seemed their colleagues were considered high potential, receiving promotions and opportunities to advance—even those with less experience, skill, and results. *Was there some secret formula known only to a privileged few?*

What they didn't realize was that their work ethic and high standards were likely the very things keeping them from what they wanted most. By consistently keeping their head down and focusing solely on producing high-quality work, their potential to excel at higher levels was not readily visible to upper management.

The shift from excellent performance to demonstrating potential is a vital component in most corporate careers. Yet it can be easy to miss, especially for those who thrive on clear goals, concrete results, and doing what's asked of them. After all, most of the time, the criteria for strong performance are clearly laid out in the job description, the annual review, and the tasks your boss tells you to do on a daily basis. Not to mention that performance is important, even essential. It's the basis for determining compensation and a prerequisite for keeping a job.

Future potential, on the other hand, is qualitative and hard to measure. How it's defined can differ for each stakeholder. Yet it's what matters most when senior managers decide who to promote to the next level.

Human Resources often uses a 9-Box Talent Grid to visualize their assessment of employee performance versus potential. This framework helps HR teams and managers identify high-potential leaders, address skill gaps, and plan succession strategies effectively. While each organization may have a different name for each box, their decisions about whether to further develop employees (and how) for each part of the grid are likely to be consistent.

For example, if most employees are clustered in the bottom left boxes, it may be time for a team upgrade. If some are in the upper right box, they need to find ways to develop and stretch those individuals.

9 BOX TALENT GRID

	LOW ← PERFORMANCE → HIGH	
POTENTIAL GEM (Develop)	HIGH POTENTIAL (Develop/Stretch)	EXCEPTIONAL (Stretch)
INCONSISTENT PLAYER (Observe)	CORE PLAYER (Maintain)	HIGH PERFORMER (Stretch/Develop)
UNDER PERFORMER (Observe/ Terminate)	AVERAGE PERFORMER (Observe)	SOLID PERFORMER (Trust)

POTENTIAL — LOW / HIGH (vertical axis)

LOW ←————— PERFORMANCE —————→ HIGH

The key to the 9-Box Grid is that a person's potential must be clearly visible to those making decisions. A sincere worker bee who turns in quality work but hardly says a word in meetings will likely be placed squarely in the "core player" box—where they'll likely stay until they switch gears.

Now, in case you think senior managers are an evil bunch trying to keep good people from advancing, keep in mind that they're busy with their own work, careers, and personal challenges. They may even find it hard to pinpoint what it is they're looking for or articulate potential when they see it.

I know because I was one of those senior managers behind closed doors, deciding who would get promoted and who wouldn't. There were strong performers on my team whom

I couldn't see taking over my role when I moved up. On the other hand, there was someone two levels down whom I could envision running the entire bank one day. But I didn't figure out my brain's rational litmus test for determining someone's potential to succeed until much later in my career (thankfully, I'll share it with you in Chapter 9).

I've Been There

Unlike many of my colleagues, I didn't come from a corporate background. My family was made up of doctors, academics, and government officials—good people who helped others and did the right thing. Their example taught me that integrity and success aren't mutually exclusive. But, as my 24-year rise to chief operating officer (COO) of an investment banking firm proved, it's not always easy. That's why my mission now is to help you navigate these waters without the suffering I experienced.

Like many others, my first couple of promotions came as part of the natural progression, even though I totally sweated them and worked harder than I probably needed to, not wanting to take anything for granted or leave it to chance.

In retrospect, those early years were the "easy" part from an advancement perspective. The requirements along the path to promotion were clearly signposted. All any of us had to do was work hard, follow instructions, and not mess up.

But in the middle years, the path got murkier. The steps to follow were no longer well marked, and miles of uncharted territory stretched ahead. On top of that, I had started a family and was doing my level best to be a good mother, daughter, sister, and wife.

It was as if I were no longer visible when it came to promotions. All I had to latch on to were vague messages: "you need to show executive presence ... be more commercially savvy ... be seen as a thought leader." I had no idea what that presence, savvy, and thought leadership looked like, much less how to develop it.

I experienced firsthand the disappointment of being left behind by peers who seemed to lead charmed lives. It was as if they had some career "snowplow" clearing the path for them. They drove ahead without so much as a speed bump. I studied them, looking for clues as to what they might be doing to warrant their rise.

One of my peers, let's call him Harry, was especially gifted at speaking up at meetings. Armed with a boatload of confidence, he practically held court when it was his turn to speak. And boy did he know who the power base was in those meetings, because he never failed to brown-nose them. To be fair, Harry was the biggest revenue producer; he also had the numbers to back up his talk. At the time, I didn't focus on that because I was too busy summing him up as a lazy smooth talker, an empty suit. What he had, however, were people skills. He knew what the powers that be were looking for at that time.

Harry got away with leaving way before I did and still received the praise, promotions, and pay raises. And Tom and Stu, two others who curried favor, spent half the day gossiping and trash-talking but still managed to pull in deals. I couldn't believe they had time to take breaks and pal around when there was work to do and clients to call.

Me, I stayed until eight or nine each evening, fielding calls from my husband, who was concerned about my welfare. It didn't seem fair that I had just as good a résumé, if not better, than any of these guys. I got better grades in school and worked twice as hard as they did, but they were getting ahead faster than I was. Were they just better at the job and able to do it quicker? What was I missing?

I shouldn't have been surprised, but it hurt when Harry got promoted and I didn't. It felt like a slap in the face because he'd joined the firm after I did and now was my senior—and that's before I knew that in just a few months I would be reporting to him. I felt positively sick to my stomach.

I felt like a loser, looking in from the outside. Work appeared easy for my colleagues while I lived in an alternate reality, working hard because "hard work always pays off." I had sacrificed too much to risk my career by taking shortcuts or cutting corners, but there had to be a better way. I simply didn't know what it was.

What I didn't realize then was the importance of visibility from two perspectives. First, making myself visible to key stakeholders, especially regarding my potential to succeed at the next level. Second, understanding the hidden rules and power dynamics of the organization. Both types of visibility are vital, and when they work together, you'll advance more quickly and easily.

Among the things I wrestled with was learning to do self-promotion without feeling I was selling my soul (or used cars) and speaking up in meetings when I felt intimidated by my peers. Because, truly, that's what I thought separated *them* from me. I was on my own with no one to bounce my ideas off of, and it felt like it took forever to get beyond the middle ranks. When I tell you I made plenty of mistakes, don't assume I'm being humble. I made more expensive mistakes than I can cover in one book.

With all the mistakes I've made in my career, I knew that my clients loved me, which was a big part of the job, but I was terrible at self-promotion, especially in internal meetings where I felt inadequate relative to my peers. I sensed this was part of the problem, an element of the game I wasn't playing. Our daily morning meetings felt like a forum for my peers to strut their stuff and brag about their accomplishments while I sat in the corner feeling like I would never measure up. I'd spend the whole meeting beating myself up for not having anything intelligent to say. With the jungle of negative self-talk I'd have to machete through, it was a miracle if I said anything at all. That negative self-talk had to be managed if I was going to make it in the industry.

I continued to spot the lessons. One of the firm's high-est-profile clients was coming in. It was crunch time. The team leader assigned me the task of analyzing comparable deals and handed me a pile of prospectuses, which I had no prior experience with. I could grind with the best of them, but this task required more than grinding. I was in uncharted territory but was too proud to ask for help and tried to figure it out on my own. By the time the team lead came to check on my work, I'd reviewed only one and a half of the deals and had no hope of finishing the analysis. It was clear I had failed the team. This was the first sign that I was going to need to develop this particular business skill—analyzing comps—or I would fall way behind.

Not even ten minutes into the meeting, the client asked for the missing details, which meant the team never asked for my help again. Mistakes like that can take you down, particularly if word gets around. But let me reassure you, you can make mistakes, even a lot of mistakes, and still succeed in your career.

Yes, the lack of specific skills was something that could hold me back, but fearing mistakes would prove even more dangerous. It's easy to be so afraid of making missteps, particularly in a high-stakes, unforgiving industry. But fear of mistakes keeps you small. As I eventually learned, it's something you must overcome to rise to the C-suite. It all goes back to self-management skills ... of showing up in a powerful way to instill confidence in those watching.

Each new mistake showed me an area I needed to develop. It took me a while to realize that no one was going to help me learn what I needed to learn; I had to invest in my own education. They would let me sink or swim, so I had to find the pool and the teacher. This is why I wrote this book and created Career Mastery™, my professional growth and success membership, both of which provide the practical strategies, tools, and actionable steps I wish I had as I navigated my career. Just as in martial arts, mastery isn't a one-time goal you achieve; it's the process of continuously working on your skills to improve.

Eventually, I recognized what I needed to learn: how to work with others in a way that demonstrated leadership; how to work on the business by honing my strategic capabilities; and how to work on myself so I could speak up and feel confident. I knew I couldn't fall into the trap of becoming lopsided in my approach because I'd already done that by focusing solely on working on the day-to-day tasks of the business and letting the other important elements fall through the cracks.

When I finally arrived in the C-suite, it meant more than just the trappings of a larger office on the management floor (what we called the "gold coast"—mahogany-lined walls, famous artwork, thick carpets, and people speaking in hushed tones). Suddenly, I had access to insider insights. I knew what was *really* going on. For once, I could enjoy the luxury of thinking about the future direction of the firm and how to position the business against competitive challenges, traveling in higher-level circles of business leaders, and having the network of people and resources to make it all happen. That's where the real opportunity to add value and make a difference lived.

It's easy to forget that we don't just wake up one morning and step into the C-suite fully formed, particularly in a famously cutthroat industry. We make a bunch of mistakes and learn lessons long before we're ready to step into that kind of role.

In an ideal world, we would all sail through our careers by demonstrating to the right people (the decision-makers and the influencers) that we've got what it takes when it matters—that we've got potential. Yet, in my own case and through my work with talented achievers, I've discovered that it's all too easy to miss those opportunities to demonstrate your potential. When you do, career progress can slow or even plateau without you ever realizing it. Yes, even when you're eminently qualified and work harder than everyone else. You may find this to be the case for you, too.

But don't think that my path or anyone else's is smooth. There is no express elevator to the top floor. There will always be challenges to overcome and mistakes to be made. The important thing is to learn and use those experiences to get stronger. Just don't let your fear of mistakes keep you playing small.

Good People Can Finish First

You're probably familiar with the giant hamster wheel: run hard only to stay in place. The middle of my career felt a lot like that wheel. Worse yet, I found it equally challenging to stay on it as to jump off and risk being left behind. But much like other areas in my life, whenever faced with two unattractive alternatives—in this case, run until I collapse or simply give up—my instinct tells me, "There has to be a better way."

I finally figured out the "better way" over twenty-four challenging years in my career and as an executive coach helping talented professionals navigate the challenges that come along with even the most successful careers.

My goal is to help good people—those who work hard, care about others, and always strive to do the right thing—achieve success at work and in life. I struggle with the old adage, "Good guys finish last." I want to live in a world where good people can and do succeed and even finish first. Because we spend most of our waking hours at work, I focus on careers. Work can be the source of great impact and enjoyment, but it often comes with *unnecessary* struggle, and I mean to alleviate that.

If you're one of the good ones, I'm all in to help you find your path forward, to develop skills that will allow you to believe in yourself and demonstrate the kind of confidence needed to win in your career and in life ... without selling your soul.

Chances are good you're like most of my clients and feel trapped between two unappealing choices: either "play the game" (and compromise your values) or "keep your head down" (and remain overlooked). This false dichotomy keeps too many talented professionals stuck.

But there is another (a better) way.

Carve Your Own Path to Success

You don't have to stoop to being an "empty suit" who "brown-noses" your way to the top, nor do you need to keep grinding out the work without recognition.

You can develop the skills and demonstrate the potential that will allow you to do this *your* way. These skills will help you navigate office politics while being yourself. They will highlight your capabilities and make *your true potential* visible to the stakeholders essential to your advancement. Because when it's all said and done, you *must* do it your way. Your natural strengths, tendencies, and values are the surest way to achieve your career (and life) ambitions without all the struggle and without selling your soul.

It's like woodworking, where you need to go *with* the grain, the natural direction of the fibers of the wood, or the wood will splinter. The same is true for your career. No matter your occupation, you will face challenges common to all, including politics. After all, the very act of proving you've got what it takes, of signaling your potential to the powers that be, is politics. So, you will have to figure out how to meet those challenges and come out on top.

You have to take ownership of your own career. You can't wait for your managers to do it for you. They won't help you manage yourself and your negative internal dialogue. They won't teach you how to better deal with your peers and the power structure. They likely won't spot the business skills needed to get to the next level until it's way too late.

Success requires you to be intentional about identifying what you need to shore up and when. And unless you want to waste years and countless promotions figuring out how to make the system work *for* rather than against you, you'll also need a solid roadmap.

Building on my own experience and work with hundreds of professionals, I've discovered there are three essential domains for career advancement: self, people, and business skills. When you have the formula for understanding the core capabilities of each and how they underpin every successful career, you pave the way for success on your own terms.

My approach has helped my coaching clients get promoted and hit the ground running in their new roles as law firm partners, heads of business units, and CEOs (to name a few). The skill-building, career-navigating framework I'm about to share with you can help you, as well, advance in your career with less stress, more ease, and greater certainty.

You only have so many hours in a day. My wish for you is to spend less of it worrying, to make fewer unnecessary mistakes than I did. I hope you invest your precious time, energy, and life force wisely. Instead of wasting them worrying about what to do next, focus on carving your own path. The following pages will show you how.

By the end of this book, you will have *clarity* on what to do next, *confidence* to carve your own path by developing yourself, and *courage* to take action to achieve the next level of success in your career ... without working yourself into the ground or selling your soul.

In other words, you will be able to master your career, so it won't master you.

As with all things in life, you get what you put into it. It's up to you to do the work. How do you do that? For the answer, you'll need to turn the page. But I promise you this: the path forward isn't about working harder—it's about working differently. And this book is your roadmap.

1

THE CAREER ADVANCEMENT ROADMAP

I still remember the day. It was seven p.m. on a Friday night, and I was one of a handful of people still in the office. My boss came to my desk and asked if I had a few minutes to talk. Then, she led me to her boss's office. One look at their faces, and I knew it couldn't be good.

"We're so sorry, but you're not going to be promoted this year. We went to bat for you, but it's a tough year, and we couldn't push it through the committee."

Turns out, most of the committee didn't even know who I was ("May who?") and those who did still saw me as a "junior bear" lacking the gravitas and presence of an executive director. I couldn't possibly have delivered the stellar performance my managers reported (or so they thought) since I had only been in the department for six months. So, the verdict was, "She can wait for another year."

This is when it dawned on me that the months and years of keeping my head down, of doing excellent work and not making waves, had run their course as a strategy. I needed to become known to decision-makers and influencers, and visible to senior managers beyond my unit. Developing external client relationships was my job, but I needed to cultivate career-enhancing relationships with movers and shakers internally, as well. I needed to understand the politics, develop allies with greater clout in the organization, and demonstrate that I had what it takes to succeed at the next level. All of which required new skills.

I spent the next several years mapping out the path to career success that I'm about to share with you. Before diving into the details, however, it's important you prepare for the road ahead...

Keep Your Eyes on Your Destination

Let's get this hard truth out of the way right off the bat: there's a huge amount of stress in the workplace. We live in a world marked by rapid change, global economic and political uncertainty, growing complexity, and the fear of AI displacing the jobs of knowledge workers. According to the 2024 Work Trend Index Annual Report from Microsoft and LinkedIn, 45% of workers globally are concerned that AI will make their jobs obsolete.[1]

Add the absence of meaningful career opportunities, increased responsibility without commensurate pay, and the perceived stress of taking on senior leadership roles, and burnout is only a blink away.

No wonder, according to Gallup's 2023 "State of the Global Workplace" report, 59% of the global workforce consists of quiet quitters—people who put no more effort into their jobs than absolutely necessary—and 77% of the global workforce are disengaged or highly disengaged.[2]

It can be a real problem when it comes to the complexities surrounding performance and potential, too. Good, hardworking achievers are more likely to give up when they can't figure out how to get ahead and don't want to risk burnout trying to do the seemingly impossible.

Don't let this be you. You have the roadmap in your hands. Sure, there may be speed bumps; you may take a detour or two, but don't give up. Keep your eyes on your destination, and you will arrive.

Understand the General Direction

What senior decision-makers are looking for goes far beyond your ability to perform specific tasks well. Whether preparing a legal brief, creating client presentations, or (in my case) analyzing financial deals, they're evaluating your potential to operate effectively at the next level.

Specifically, they're looking for your potential in three main areas:

1. **Working with people:** The way you interact with others matters since none of us succeeds on our own.

2. **Working on the business:** The ability to deliver results matters whether you're in a business, non-profit, higher education, or government setting.

3. **Working on your self:** Understanding yourself and being able to bring out your best regardless of the situation as the foundation for your success in your career and life.

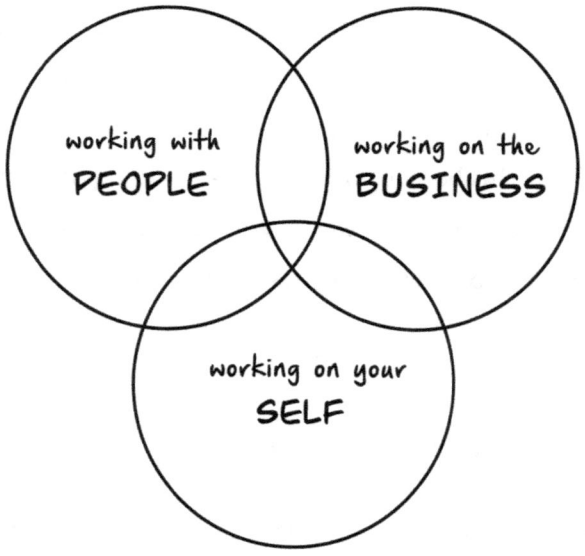

As you can see from the illustration, they're interrelated. Your strengths in one area can help you build your potential in the other areas. For example, being self-aware (a Self skill) will help you become a better leader for your team (a People skill), and being an effective communicator (a People skill) will help you get people on board and therefore drive superior business results (a Business skill). And being strategic (a Business skill) will help you build your personal brand and profile (a Self skill).

Since one of the areas will come more naturally to you than the others, don't fall into the trap of becoming lopsided in your approach. You'll want to ensure you're building your career muscles in all three areas. Being over-reliant on one or two areas has stopped many achievers from advancing beyond a certain point in their careers.

To keep you grounded and ready for whatever lies ahead, this book is organized according to these areas.

Remember: You're in the Driver's Seat

Unless you lead a truly charmed life, where your desires are anticipated and handed to you on a silver platter, you will reach a point in your career when you have to take ownership if you want to achieve your career goals.

For most of the people I've mentored and coached over the years, this realization tends to occur mid-career when they bump up against the politics and pressures that lead to a feeling of dissatisfaction. So, if this is how you're feeling, you are (as my mother would say) "nothing but normal."

This is where, if you want to advance, the right people need to see that you have the potential to take on and succeed at the next level. Again, these are the senior decision-makers and the people who influence them. We'll talk more about them in Chapter 2 on stakeholders.

So, how do you make your potential visible? It depends on what's required at the next level, your strengths, and what areas you need to work on.

The key is to be regularly working on the skills that demonstrate your potential in all three areas. All of them are relevant throughout your career; however, they will look different and vary in importance at each stage. For example, back when you were starting out in your career, having presence was simply showing up and looking the part in a meeting. But mid-career, the expectations are much higher. You're expected to have that elusive "executive presence." Keep progressing to even more senior levels, and it becomes about gravitas and "commanding the room."

At any point in your career, there will be a few areas that are more important to work on than others. Again, this will depend on where you are already strong versus where you need to develop. The point is you need to take charge (versus waiting for someone else to develop you). Don't worry; that's what the roadmap is all about—helping you get it done.

Think in Terms of Components

Not only are there three main areas that indicate potential, but each also contains three components that you will want to develop for career success:

1. Working with People

    •   Stakeholder Management

- Building and Maintaining a High-Performing Team
- Getting Your Point Across and Influencing

2. Working on the Business

- Recognizing Opportunities and Charting New Directions
- Taking Action Despite Uncertainty
- Transitioning from Caretaker to Rainmaker

3. Working on Your Self

- Understanding and Managing Yourself
- Showing Up as Your Best Self and Being Visible
- Investing in Your Community of Supporters

Each of these nine components represents a distinct skill set. Develop them together, and you'll create a powerful foundation for career advancement. They are the elements that senior leaders consistently look for when identifying high-potential talent. These are also the skills that my Career Mastery membership helps you develop and demonstrate.

Stay Focused

You'll be overwhelmed if you try to focus on too many areas at once. So, you need to find the "right mix." What do you need to develop and demonstrate to others right now? It could be shoring up an area of weakness or filling in a gap in your skills. It might be leveraging an area where you're already strong or following your instincts on what feels most energizing.

Whatever you determine the "right mix" to be, the 80/20 rule is likely to apply. This rule states that the biggest step change in your results (the 80%) will be driven by improvements you make to a small subset (the 20%). So instead of working on nine things at the same time, identify the one or two skills that could make the biggest difference to your progress if you were to focus on them right now.

When you narrow down your focus and work on specific areas, you'll be in a much better position to prove you've got what it takes when the opportunity arises—even if you're not fully aware of the opportunity.

So, start with one or two areas that will move the needle most for you right now, and focus on those. We've included an assessment in the resources section (www.thevisiblebook. com/resources) to help you identify which areas to prioritize. The more you work on them, the better you'll become, and the more natural they will be. Then you'll be on your way to creating a virtuous cycle that can lift your career onward and upward.

Use the Roadmap as a Reference

The following pages will explore:

- The core elements of each skill and why they matter for your advancement

- Real-world examples of how it looks when done well (and what happens when it's not)

- Common obstacles and pitfalls that can derail your progress

- Practical strategies and action steps to develop each skill

- Personal Action Plans to help you apply what you've learned immediately

And the conclusion helps you synthesize everything into your next bold moves to accelerate your career progress.

Keep in mind, this is not a "one and done" scenario. What you need to demonstrate right now will continually change throughout your career. You'll want to return to these areas over and over again. This is how you develop in an increasingly advanced and nuanced way, progressing to higher levels of excellence as you advance in your career.

As the roadmap, you'll likely need to refer to the following pages on multiple occasions. Feel free to skip around to the chapter that makes the most sense for you. You don't need to read the book in order. Give yourself permission to focus on the areas that are right for you in the moment. Skim the chapters that are areas of strength and focus on the ones you want to work on.

Enjoy the Journey

As you explore your career and these key areas, avoid thinking of them as assignments. This is not some school paper that you turn in and never look at again. These are living, breathing skills that you need to keep fresh. They need to evolve based on your growing maturity, the changing dynamics and goals of your organization, and the aspects of your career that are most exciting, creative, and rewarding for you.

Think of it more along the lines of play. The more actively you engage with this work, the more success and ease you'll enjoy. In the words of a recent client, "It's fun when things pan out!"

The path I'm outlining isn't just about career advancement; it's about finding greater satisfaction and purpose in your work. When you demonstrate your potential in the three key areas—working with people, working on the business, and working on your self – you not only position yourself for promotion, but you also create a more fulfilling professional experience along the way.

And now, it's time for you to jump in so you can have more fun and success with your career, too.

PART 1

WORKING
WITH
PEOPLE

2

MANAGING YOUR STAKEHOLDERS

Winning Support Without Playing Politics

In real estate, it's all about "location, location, location." When it comes to managing your stakeholders, it's all about relationship, relationship, relationship. Fortunately, this doesn't mean you need to be such close pals that your families vacation together. But it does mean building some constructive connections. To do that, it helps to tune in to human behavior and what makes people tick (including yourself, which we'll cover in more detail in Chapter 8).

That's why, looking back, I credit all my stakeholder management abilities to a course I took in high school. That's right; it wasn't a course from my economics degree from Harvard or my MBA from Harvard Business School. It was a course from my public education in New Jersey. Behavioral Sciences, taught by Ms. Brick, was an intro to psychology course for high school juniors. It explained so much about why certain classmates clashed with the math teacher but not the English teacher, and how to propose an idea in a way that would make my parents more likely to agree.

These same behavioral findings hold in the workplace. For example, it helps to understand that your boss will likely be upset if you bring an idea or complaint to *their* boss without a heads-up; how to go about getting in front of that skip-level boss gracefully, without upsetting your direct boss in the process; and that the technology project you're working on is more likely to succeed if you've already built a trusted relationship with the powerful sales and product development teams, from whom you'll need support (bring them into the picture early on so they can help shape the solution instead of possibly vetoing it when it's sprung on them at the end).

By mid-career, success depends on impressing and influencing a diverse group of stakeholders, not simply your boss. Your ability to advance now hinges on how effectively you navigate this expanded network of relationships. In fact, the more senior you become, the more you get things done through others rather than contributing value on your own (we'll talk about this more in Chapter 3 about leading teams). There's a widening circle of people who are involved with or affected by what you do beyond your boss. You need to have them on board to deliver business results for you to be seen as having the potential to do more and keep advancing.

Stakeholders, as this circle of people is known, care about and have a say in what you do, how you do it, and how well you're perceived to be doing it. Because of their influence on your projects and career outcomes, it's worth being intentional about building and managing stakeholder relationships, whether they're internal or external to your organization—even if you don't particularly like each other.

Recognizing Your Stakeholders

It's worth pointing out that just because someone is a stakeholder doesn't make them an automatic fan or supporter. That's because most of the time, you don't get to choose who your stakeholders are. You're thrust together in a work setting and need to figure out how to make it work. Take your boss, for example. They clearly have a stake in what you do and how well you do it. They're also someone whose opinion counts when it comes to judging your performance and potential. But while they matter a lot to your career, they could be a jerk who's actively trying to undermine you (hopefully not, but it can happen).

So, your stakeholders are not the same as your network of supporters. In an ideal world, there's a great deal of overlap, but that's not always the case. Cultivating your network of relationships is so vital that we devote an entire chapter to this skill (Chapter 10). For now, let's return to your stakeholders.

Your key stakeholders at the mid-career level are still likely to be primarily internal, which includes your reporting line (boss, plus one to two levels up), immediate team members, and key colleagues in other product areas, geographical regions, support services areas, and functional areas (e.g., finance, legal, sales, operations, HR, marketing). External stakeholders would include any external clients you may have and, of course, your family.

However, as you advance to senior management and C-suite levels, you'll need to manage a much broader range of internal and external stakeholders, including the board, employees, customers, suppliers, the press, and regulators—just to name a few.

Your stakeholder group shifts with each new role or change in responsibilities. They may also change because other parts of the organization change, whether through reorganizations, departures, or promotions. It's easy to overlook stakeholder shifts during periods of transition, especially when you're taking on new responsibilities and your attention is focused on learning your new job. Therefore, it's essential to review who those stakeholders may be regularly.

Not All Stakeholders Are Created Equal

Before you worry about the huge task of keeping track of all these people, understand that they're not all equally important. Some will be primary while others will be secondary or even tertiary. If a stakeholder is vital to your ability to do what you do or has the power to approve or veto your proposals, they're primary stakeholders. The way to triage is based on how important your work is to each other and their power to approve, endorse, or veto.

Do not confuse visibility with importance. Just because you don't see a particular stakeholder very often doesn't mean they're secondary. This was the mistake I made with my sales and trading counterparts when I first moved to the London office; they turned out to have a significant voice in determining how I was perceived.

Build on What You Already Know

If the idea of managing stakeholders sounds daunting, don't worry. You have a lot of experience in stakeholder management already, so you're not starting from scratch.

As a toddler, your parents and others in your household all had a stake in your growth and development. Because you relied on them to get what you needed to survive and thrive, you had to get good at figuring out who controlled which decisions and what they cared about most. The better you were at figuring out what made them tick, the more you were able to get what you wanted—like knowing which parent was more likely to give you extra spending money or how to get Uncle Rocky to buy you that candy you weren't supposed to have.

In other words, they were the first stakeholders you managed.

Today, your personal life rides on knowing the preferences and tendencies of your partner or friends. Knowing which friend gets upset when you're late, for example, or that your partner's pet peeve is having dishes piled up in the sink can help you maintain good relationships.

You can draw on these same skills to help you manage your relationships with stakeholders in your work and career. It's about understanding the people you work with and handling your relationships with them successfully. It's about navigating the politics gracefully and effectively.

In case you think we're heading toward playing office politics like the typical stuffed shirt intent on brown-nosing the boss, rest assured that's not what I'm talking about. My favorite definition of politics comes from my mother, who, as a pediatrician, had ample opportunity to observe interactions between children and others—from friends to family members. "Politics is simply what happens when there are two or more people involved. It's a little society." And every society has its culture, norms, conflicts, and ways to get along.

In the context of work and career, consider this a helpful reminder: you are not operating in isolation; instead, you are part of a "little society" (your team or unit) within a broader ecosystem (your organization and beyond). I invite you to reframe "playing office politics" as understanding your wider audience and their care and feeding. This will make it far more energizing and doable.

And keep in mind, when you manage stakeholder relationships effectively, you create a reinforcing cycle of mutual success. Your stakeholders begin to advocate for your work because they see how it benefits them, which opens more doors for your initiatives. As your reputation grows, you gain greater influence to support their priorities too. This reciprocal dynamic replaces the common zero-sum approach, where one person's win feels like another's loss. Instead, your stakeholders become invested in your success because they recognize it contributes to their own.

When you master the skill of stakeholder management, you will have become adept at "navigating the politics" essential to your career success, and you will have done it without being political. There's no need to sacrifice your values to get ahead or suck up to someone who makes you sick to your stomach.

So, let's talk about what stakeholder management looks like when it's done well.

Stakeholder Management Done Well

My client Charles excels at stakeholder management and has a much easier time getting the best outcomes for his team and projects than his peers. Charles knows (and is known to) his key stakeholders across the organization, which paves the way for projects and requests to move smoothly through the internal approval process. Key people feel comfortable that they will not be "blindsided" or surprised by what Charles and his team are doing.

That's because Charles keeps in touch with them regularly—an update email here and there, a quick fly-by hello as he's passing someone's office, an invitation to join a client meeting, a semiannual coffee to get advice on his business strategy, and so forth.

Through these interactions, he has figured out the what, when, and how of keeping in touch with each individual. He does so in a way that's suited to their interests and needs, while being relatively easy for him. And since he took the time to build these connections, if something falls through the cracks, he has sufficient relationship chits to recover and get back on track.

Stakeholder Management Done Poorly

Sam, on the other hand, was a star on the investment bank's trading desk. He had gone to one of the "right schools." He was considered exceptionally bright among a firm of exceptionally bright people. Not only that, but Sam also had an uncanny sense of the markets for which he was responsible. As a result, he was consistently the biggest producer on the desk and was ultimately put in charge of the unit.

Sam and his team saw themselves as a money-making engine that didn't need the other divisions to accomplish their goals. In Sam's view, if other divisions ran their businesses the way he ran his, the shareholders would be better off. Sam aspired to be part of the firm's top management team one day. However, once Sam was promoted to head the unit, he needed to interact directly with the other areas of the firm, without his extremely diplomatic division head running interference.

Given his mindset, Sam soon developed a terrible reputation with the client relationship teams in other areas of the organization. They complained about his disregard for their interests as well as his refusal to engage in constructive dialogue to resolve issues. No wonder. Sam thought they were dopes and wasn't interested in cooperating or collaborating. He was convinced they had nothing to add.

In the end, his smarter-than-thou attitude was his downfall. Sam failed to understand that to reach the lofty positions he aspired to, he needed the support of people in the other divisions, especially in those closed-door meetings where senior management positions were determined. Even his previously supportive boss had to admit he could no longer push for Sam's advancement, and Sam ultimately left the firm.

How could such a brilliant intellect miss the importance of managing his stakeholder relationships? In retrospect, it seems that he didn't even recognize that they were stakeholders.

Now, let's get practical and bring it back to you.

Putting Stakeholder Management into Practice

Whatever stage you're at in your career, there are things you can do to create the stakeholder relationships you need and manage them well:

Step 1: Identify your stakeholders.

While it may sound simple to identify your stakeholders, it can be more complicated than you think. Even well-meaning people can make the career-limiting mistake of overlooking an entire group of stakeholders, so you want to get this right. One overlooked group could spell trouble—if ignored, they can come out of the shadows and bite you when you least expect it.

When senior management transferred me to London to start a new business unit, my marching orders were to put together a business plan, build a team, and, most importantly, get the European relationship bankers on board because they were our entry point to the corporate client base. Without the bankers, we could not succeed.

I was to leverage my reputation with U.S.-based bankers, as well as our European colleagues. I had, after all, spent the first decade of my career earning their trust and support. Of course, we could work together to build the new business. I understood how the system worked. This would generate a new stream of revenue from our banking clients, which, in turn, would generate products for the firm's sales and trading unit to sell to investors.

Armed with a list of our bankers in Europe, I sat down with my colleagues in the U.S. to figure out who the opinion leaders were—the ones with the biggest clients, the "friendlies" versus the skeptics. This prioritization meant I could figure out who to reach out to first—who were the 20% who were likely to deliver 80% of the business opportunities.

Within the first 90 days of landing in London, I had met with all the top bankers and felt good about getting the most important part of my assignment underway. Little did I know that I had failed to recognize an important set of stakeholders, which threatened to undermine any success I hoped to achieve.

One day, my boss called me into his office. My counterparts in sales and trading were grumbling about me. Six months had gone by, and as far as they could tell, I hadn't done a thing to justify my existence in London. They questioned, "When is she going to start pulling her own weight?" Some even advocated for me to be shipped back to New York.

That's when it hit me. I had taken my assignment too literally, spending all my time with the relationship bankers without ever meeting with most of the sales and trading leaders. They were paying for half of my business unit but had been left out of the loop, leaving it to their imagination as to what the hell I was doing all day. And when the human brain lacks information, it makes something up, usually with worst-case thinking.

They were like the 13th slighted fairy in Grimm's *Sleeping Beauty* tale—the one who wasn't invited to the royal christening but crashed the party to put a curse on the princess, causing her to sleep for one hundred years before being awakened by a handsome prince. In my case, it was "shape up or be gone," and there was no handsome prince to save me.

So don't forget the 13th fairy equivalent. Consider the people you may have missed. In fact, assume you've missed some. Revisit your list from time to time because things change, and every time you have a new project or role, different stakeholders may come into the frame or fade away.

Step 2: Make a list.

List out the top five to ten people who have an interest in, are affected by, or can affect what you do and don't do (you can add to this later, but start with at least five). They can be internal or external to your organization, but their buy-in is crucial to your success. If you don't know who they are, ask someone you trust who is politically savvy, and think about these categories:

- People who can green-light your project or kill it
- People who can accelerate your progress
- People who can set you back
- People who can amplify what you do or recommend you to others

- People who pay and promote you

- People who recognize you for your performance

The simplest way to do this is to write your list wherever you like to take notes, whether that's a clean sheet of paper, a notebook, a tablet, or a computer.

If you're a visual learner, this template might appeal to you. You can download a free editable copy at www.thevisible-book.com/resources.

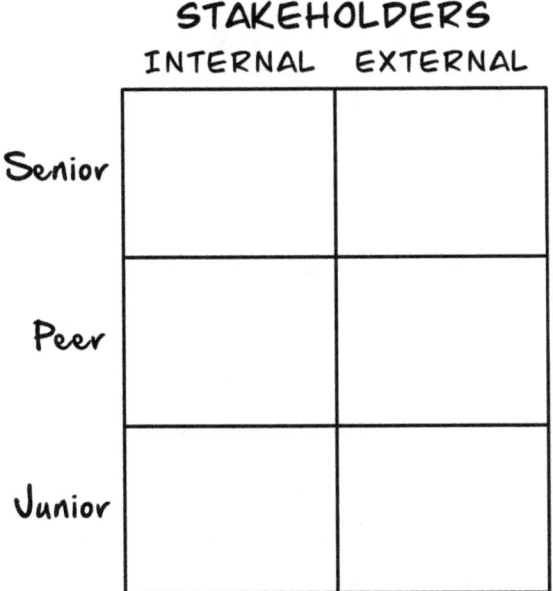

Step 3: Map them out.

Now that you have your list of key stakeholders, it's time to step back and assess them—because not all stakeholders are created equal. Some will be more important than others, and mapping them out will help you decide where to focus your time, energy, and attention.

You probably have a gut feeling for whom you need to spend more time with, but adding some rigor to the analysis may bring a few surprises. In my case, mapping out my stakeholders after feedback from my boss showed me just how much work I needed to do.

By the end of this step, you'll have a visual map of where you stand with your key stakeholders in a way that will give you clarity on where to focus your efforts. You'll want to assess each of your key stakeholders on two dimensions:

1. **How much impact do they have on your career (or business)?** You don't need to get too scientific about it—high, medium, or low will do. This is simply the first cut. You can always change it later.

2. **How strong is your relationship?** Rate your relationship from strong to weak. Note: you get to decide how to define "weak" relationships, whether that's not knowing who you are or, worse yet, knowing who you are but having a negative impression.

Then, based on your assessment, plot your key stakeholders in the relevant quadrant of the Stakeholder Map. For a downloadable version of this stakeholder map that you can fill out online, see the resources page (www.thevisiblebook.com/resources).

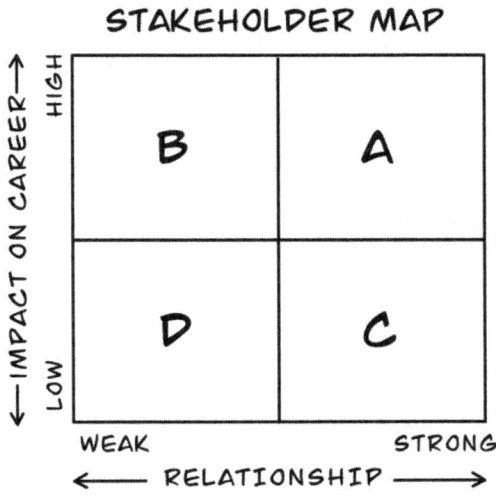

- **Quadrant A:** These are people who have a significant impact on your career and with whom you have a strong relationship. This could be your manager, skip-level manager, or senior sponsor who advocates for you behind closed doors. A sponsor is someone more senior who actively advocates for you, especially in closed-door discussions about promotions and opportunities. Unlike mentors who provide advice, sponsors use their influence to create opportunities for you. (We'll talk more about sponsors in Chapter 10.) Quadrant A is where you're in great shape, and it's all about maintaining the relationship and leveraging it.

- **Quadrant B:** These are stakeholders who have a significant impact on your career, but your relationship is weak or non-existent. This is where you will want to do some work.

- **Quadrant C:** These stakeholders know, like, and respect you but don't have as much influence on your career as the people in quadrants A and B. While they have less direct power to improve your career and business outcomes, they are an asset you can leverage.

- **Quadrant D:** You probably won't have many stakeholders in this category, and they aren't a priority unless they are likely to become Bs in the future. As my mother always advised, "Be kind to everyone. You never know who might become important to you one day."

Step 4: Decide where to focus.

Start by looking at your map at a distance, like those eye tests where you stand ten feet away and see what letters you recognize. Are your stakeholders all bunched up in one quadrant, or are they scattered across several? Where is the greatest concentration? If most are in quadrant A, that's great news. If you have mostly B's (like I did when I first landed in London), you have your work cut out for you.

The main idea is to move as many of your B's into quadrant A as you can. That is, cultivate your relationships with the most influential stakeholders for your career so they become supporters.

Now zoom in to look at the specific names on your map and choose the top two to three you would like to focus on for the next quarter. It could be someone in quadrant B, one of your A's you'd like to shift further to the right, or a combination. Circle these names.

Step 5: Create a plan.

For each of those two to three stakeholders, create a plan for what you'll do over the next three months to improve your relationships. In essence, this is the "care and feeding" of your most important stakeholders.

Here are some questions to prime your thinking and help you identify your action steps:

- What are your goals with this stakeholder, and how will you know when you've succeeded?

- What are their interests, and what can you do to help them succeed?

- What are their concerns, and how can you address them?

- What do you need to keep them apprised of, and how and when is it best to communicate with them?

- What are the immediate next steps you will take, who can help you, and how will you hold yourself accountable?

Step 6: Act.

Without action, nothing will change. This step is what saved me in London, where I had neglected the "13th fairy" stakeholders in sales and trading. I was able to get these critical stakeholders on board by building relationships one by one.

Here's how I did it:

The first round of one-to-one meetings was essentially a listening tour. While most were gracious in expressing their "concerns," others were brutally honest with their complaints. Happily, even those tough meetings blossomed into relationships of mutual respect because I showed I could handle the challenge.

By the end of the quarter, we'd gotten to know each other and had come to a shared vision of what success would look like. Ultimately, we built relationships based on mutual respect and trust, which proved instrumental in ending the year with the number one position in the market. So, no matter how challenging your situation may be with your stakeholders, it pays to make the effort.

Mastering stakeholder management is one of the most visible indicators of your readiness for senior leadership roles. When you consistently build trust, navigate politics gracefully, and turn potential critics into advocates, senior executives take notice. These aren't just relationship skills—they're the foundation of executive presence and influence. The time you invest in mapping and nurturing these key relationships will pay dividends throughout your career advancement journey.

Now it's over to you. It's time to act on your plan.

PERSONAL ACTION PLAN

1. **Who are your key stakeholders right now?** List five to seven people who have a significant influence over your work success and career advancement. Include those who can approve or veto your initiatives, accelerate your progress, or amplify your reputation. (Don't overthink—you can always add more later.)

2. **Using the stakeholder map, where do your relationships stand?** Plot each stakeholder based on their impact on your career (high, medium, low) and your relationship strength (strong, weak). Which quadrant has the most names? What does this tell you about where you need to focus?

3. **Which two to three "Quadrant B" relationships (high impact, weak relationship) would make the biggest difference to your success if strengthened?** Circle these names as they are your priorities for the next quarter.

4. **For each priority stakeholder, what's your "care and feeding" strategy?** Consider: What do they care about most? How can you help them succeed? What's the best way to stay connected with them? What immediate concerns might they have about you or your work?

5. **What's one specific action you'll take this week to strengthen a key stakeholder relationship?** Be concrete. Will you send an update email, schedule a coffee meeting, invite them to a meeting, or something else? Commit to doing this consistently.

3

LEADING BEYOND A TITLE

How to Build Your Team's Trust

A mentor once told me, "At the senior leadership level, we don't need you to be the smartest person in the room. We need you to be the person who can assemble and lead a team of the smartest people in their respective areas."

It's not something you usually dive right into. For the most part, you begin your career developing technical skills and expertise in a particular subject or function. Then, you progress to leading small teams where you leverage your expertise as you develop your leadership capabilities.

As you advance into mid-career, however, your ability to create environments where diverse talent thrives often becomes more important than your technical expertise. This is where true leadership shines, because you not only build higher-performing teams but also demonstrate your potential to succeed at more senior leadership levels (though it will serve you well no matter what you do in your career).

As you begin to build and maintain a high-performance team, keep the following over-arching rules in mind...

Rule 1: Don't accept the status quo.

One of my executive coaching clients (let's call him Paul) was practically perfect in every way. He did his work to an exceptionally high standard, had a tremendous work capacity, and frankly, did everything well. Not only that, but he never complained about the gaps in his staffing and gratefully accepted the junior-level staff he was given. Paul was the greatest thing since sliced bread... or was he?

Being someone who dutifully accepted what was given to him served Paul well for the first couple of years. As he got more senior, however...

The juniors Paul had been given weren't the best of the bunch. So, when he delegated to them, he had to fix their work. That compounded the problem he faced from understaffing, which put him at his limit for "doing more with less." The net effect was that he didn't attract the best people because he tolerated mediocrity. This left Paul without a credible bench—since there was no one to take over his role, he couldn't get promoted.

Meanwhile, his boss was looking at him and wondering why he was always alone in meetings. *Where was his team?* While his output remained excellent, it didn't seem sustainable. She was afraid he'd burn out when he should be creating the next generation of leaders.

Her admiration turned into concern. She sensed a real issue in the future: was it the caliber of the team, Paul's inability to delegate and hold people accountable, his failure to spend enough time developing his people, or a mixture of all three?

As his story illustrates, accepting everything isn't actually being a team player—it's setting yourself and your team up for underperformance and even failure. Don't simply accept the status quo when it comes to your team. At the least, it will cause more work for you. At the worst, it could deliver a severe blow to your career.

Rule 2: Create an environment of psychological safety.

Before you can bring out anyone's best performance, you need to create the conditions where people feel safe to take risks, voice their opinions, and be their authentic selves. It's called psychological safety, which my classmate and Harvard Business School Professor Amy Edmondson defines as "a belief that one will not be punished or humiliated for speaking up with ideas, questions, concerns, or mistakes."[3]

Her research shows that teams with high psychological safety outperform others because team members are more likely to:

- Admit mistakes quickly so they can be fixed.

- Share information that might be uncomfortable but necessary.

- Take appropriate risks that lead to innovation.

- Ask for help when they need it.

In countless meetings, I've watched talented people sweat through discussions, clearly uncomfortable with speaking up. I've also been that person, debating with myself whether to contribute when someone else is making my point.

As a leader, you need to actively create space for everyone to participate, not simply the naturally vocal ones. As they say, still waters run deep, and the people who are observant but need more processing time may be your deepest thinkers—the ones who come up with scenarios and ideas no one else has thought of.

That's why, in the leadership programs I run, we set "rules of belonging." They include such agreements as: "We share the airtime. We take a 'yes, and' approach instead of 'no, but.' We treat each other with respect."

Once you've established the ground rules, it's crucial to enforce them. You'll likely lose all credibility if you fail to address someone who goes against the norms to which you all agreed. Your team will shut down as everyone realizes the "safe space" was merely theoretical.

Your reaction in these moments defines your leadership culture more than any mission statement ever could.

Rule 3: Treat people the way *they* want to be treated.

The human element of leadership makes it all a bit challenging. People are messy, and none are exactly the same. What works to inspire or motivate one team member can backfire with another.

We tend to adopt "the golden rule": treat people the way *you* want to be treated. Unfortunately, this will not create an atmosphere where *all* can flourish, because not all team members are going to be like you. Instead, you need to treat them as *they* want to be treated.

It's like being a gardener. The gardener's job is to provide a variety of plants with the space to grow, the right kind of soil, and enough light and water so they can flourish. As they tend the garden and keep the weeds at bay, they understand the importance of meeting the unique needs of each plant.

I do not have a green thumb. As a matter of fact, I have a bad habit of thinking *plants are plants* and giving each the same amount of water. That typically means my basil plants drown within weeks while my begonias dry out and wither.

You'll experience a similar outcome if you treat everyone on your team the same. Some people don't need much praise (they may even be embarrassed by it); others need to be recognized and encouraged regularly (and publicly). Some prefer direct feedback while others wilt from a gentle suggestion.

The key is to understand your team members as individuals and the primary drivers for each of them. This is how you'll learn their care and feeding, how you'll learn the direction, motivation, and atmosphere they need to do their best work.

In other words, figure out what brings out the best in each team member and do that. Which is a whole other book.

Rule 4: Let them know where they stand.

If you have a manager who doesn't give much feedback, it can be excruciating to try to figure out what they think of you. *Are you in their good graces or first in line to be let go? Are they frowning because they hate your proposal, or are they stressed about something totally unrelated?* It's like being back in high school and wondering if that classmate has a crush on you. So much mental energy wasted.

When you keep people wondering and worrying, you drain energy that could be pulled toward the common goal instead. That's why it's important to find ways to make it clear where people stand with you.

The best way to do that is through conversations. Engaging in "good contracting upfront" is especially important. This means setting and agreeing on expectations early on for how you want to be with one another. These guidelines or "rules of engagement" are a way to clarify what is and is not okay when it comes to interacting with each other.

This is something I do at the start of my executive coaching engagements, and I've come to see that the same approach to leadership works wonders with my teams, too. For example, I like to give and get permission from team members to share feedback regularly and in real time. This normalizes feedback in our relationship. Getting feedback early and often also allows for mid-course adjustments. This helps alleviate the damage often caused by waiting for a formal process. (Ever learn you should have done things differently at year-end, when it's too late?) For a guide on how to do good contracting upfront, see the resources page (www.thevisiblebook.com/resources).

Having permission to share feedback also makes it easier to have those tough conversations you might otherwise dread or avoid. When you have them, keep it constructive, and deliver your message "with love and grace." For example, "I appreciated the way you fielded questions X and Y—your answers were crisp, clear, and succinct. The way you presented slide Z was different, though; next time, I would love to see you take the same approach as you did for X and Y. I think you'd feel more powerful, and the communication would be more effective. I know you can do it because I saw how effective you were with X and Y. What are your thoughts?"

Just remember that there's a power differential between you and your team members. So, when the tables are turned, you may need to invite their feedback at the start. Once they give it, it's vital that you respond in a way that makes them comfortable to provide feedback again in the future.

Once you treat your team members the way they want to be treated and are clear about where they stand, you have room to help them develop and grow.

Rule 5: Invest in your people.

While technical skills can give a boost to performance, it's the qualitative skills that supercharge results over the longer term. This is especially true in a world where AI and other technological advances are changing things so fast that nonhuman skills are at risk of being made obsolete overnight.

You want (and need) your team members to be able to communicate their ideas persuasively to colleagues whose partnership is required, without your needing to intervene to get them on board or resolve conflicts. You want (and need) your team members to develop sound business judgment, so they'll make better decisions without needing your input at every turn. You want (and need) your team members to build their leadership skills, so your job as team leader will be easier, allowing you to build up your career sooner.

This is where the 70/20/10 model comes into play. Researchers Morgan McCall, Michael Lombardo, and Robert A. Eichinger, working with the Center for Creative Leadership, found that 70% of knowledge comes from job-related experiences, including tasks and problem-solving; 20% from interactions with others, including feedback, mentoring, and role models; and 10% from formal training, including reading books and articles.[4] As a team leader, consider how you might invest in your team members by strengthening their learning and development:

For the 70% on-the-job, are you assigning them projects where they can learn and grow? Are you encouraging them to come to you with proposed solutions to the problems? Which team members are ready for a "stretch assignment" that pushes them outside of their comfort zone?

For the 20% that's learning from others, are you taking advantage of teachable moments—those unplanned situations where you can share your knowledge and experience with them in real time? Who could use a little more feedback or mentoring from you? To what extent are you modeling the behavior you expect from your team? Or not?

And for the 10% formal learning, are you making sure they get to the training sessions they've signed up for? Who could you nominate for leadership programs the organization offers? Could you negotiate for a training budget for your unit (which you can benefit from, too)?

If you have a limited budget, time, and attention, the 9-Box Talent Grid from the introduction can help you determine which team members to invest in and how.

Keep Out the Worst in Yourself

We all have our own dysfunctions (micromanaging, avoiding confrontation, taking credit for the work of others, to name a few). When they raise their ugly heads, it drains productivity and creativity from the team.

Take it from me. I know.

I've always thought of myself as a great boss. I cared about my team, protected them from the politics, and advocated for their pay and promotions behind closed doors. But it turns out I had a giant blind spot. Despite the best of intentions, some of my natural tendencies were turning me into a nightmare manager, especially when I was under stress. And my job was filled with stress. At my worst, my high standards and attention to detail became insecurity and perfectionism. My perfectionism manifested as micromanagement that went well beyond helpful guidance.

In my quest to "get it right," I had my team working around the clock to research the answers to every possible question our clients might ask and produce a giant presentation deck. Half the pages had to be redone multiple times as I changed my mind on aspects such as footnotes and commas. When my juniors discovered that half of the materials they produced never got discussed in the client meetings, my reputation as a team leader took a big hit. It took four years for the complaints about my "wasting resources" to disappear from my annual evaluations, even though my behavior had changed long before that.

Here's another example: a former colleague's boss was unpredictable in the way he would respond. One day, he was the ideal caring professional who provided guidance and encouragement. The next day, he could turn into a vicious critic, accusing my colleague of mishandling a situation and berating her in front of her team. His emails were equally unpredictable—praise for a job well done followed by a "nasty-gram" a week later. ("This presentation is a piece of crap. You'll never make managing director with this kind of pathetic attempt.")

At his best, he was the ideal boss, but when his stress personality emerged, he became toxic. The impact this boss had was to keep my colleague guessing and walking on eggshells, not knowing when the next tongue-lashing would happen. She was constantly under stress, and her health began to suffer. It was only when we heard about it and encouraged her to talk to her skip-level boss that things improved. But by then, a lot of damage had been done both to my colleague's well-being and her boss's reputation.

Turns out, sometimes the best thing you can do to bring out the best in your team is keep out the worst in yourself.

Know Your Saboteurs

According to Shirzad Chamine, author of the *New York Times* bestselling *Positive Intelligence*, when we face challenges (fear or stress), our minds rely upon ten automatic responses—Saboteurs, they're called. They may judge or control, for example, try to please everyone, or avoid the situation altogether.[5]

These Saboteurs are as follows, and you can take Chamine's free Positive Intelligence® assessment to identify the ones that are most relevant for you.

- **Judge:** The master saboteur, which finds faults with yourself, others, and circumstances, leading to disappointment, anger, regret, guilt, shame, and anxiety. It activates the other saboteurs.

- **Avoider:** Focuses excessively on the positive and pleasant, avoiding difficult or unpleasant tasks and conflicts.

- **Controller:** Driven by anxiety, needs to take charge and control situations and people, leading to impatience and frustration when unable to do so.

- **Hyper-Achiever:** Bases self-worth on constant performance and achievement, quickly discounting past successes and always needing more.

- **Hyper-Rational:** Focuses intensely on rational processing, often at the expense of emotional connection, which can come off as uncaring or arrogant.

- **Hyper-Vigilant:** Experiences continuous anxiety about dangers and what could go wrong, with vigilance that never rests.

- **Pleaser:** Seeks acceptance and affection by helping or pleasing others, often losing sight of their own needs and feeling resentful as a result.

- **Restless:** Constantly seeks new excitement and activity, rarely at peace or satisfied with the present moment.

- **Stickler:** Perfectionist tendencies, needing order and organization, leading to frustration with others who don't meet their standards.

- **Victim:** Focuses on feelings of pain and disappointment, often to gain attention or affection, and can feel powerless or resentful.

What's particularly important for team leaders to understand is that these Saboteurs have a certain contagion effect. When you're operating from a place of fear, judgment, or insecurity (what Chamine calls "Saboteur mode"), you activate similar responses in your team members—as though your negative mental state is contagious.

It's this contagion effect that lands such a damaging blow to team performance. When you micromanage from your

Controller Saboteur, team members shift into their protective states. They may become passive (Avoider) or defensive (Controller). Each protective response drains an enormous amount of energy from the system—energy that could otherwise be directed toward creative work and results.

The first step to preventing this negative cycle is to recognize when you're slipping into your Saboteur patterns. This allows you to pause and reset before infecting your entire team.

Whether you're about to slip or already in the grip of a Saboteur pattern, there are steps you can take to activate what Chamine calls your Sage Brain, or the wise part of your brain. This is where you can think clearly and tap into your creativity, good judgment, and positive emotions. This, too, is contagious, but in a good way.

To shift from Saboteur to Sage, Chamine recommends "PQ Reps." These are short mental exercises designed to shift your brain activity from negative to positive.

Here are a few examples:

- **Sensory Focus** Rub your fingertips together slowly, paying attention to the sensation for ten seconds.

- **Breathing Awareness** Focus on the rhythm of your breathing as you engage in "triangle breathing": breathe in for a slow count of three; hold that breath for another count of three; and breathe out for a count of four. This resets your nervous system to bring you back to a calm state.

- **Three Gifts Exercise** Acknowledge that every situation, even the most negative ones, can be a gift and an opportunity. Reflect on three ways a negative situation could be turned into a positive outcome. For example, having your best team member quit can feel devastating. Still, it could bring the opportunity to find someone even better, the chance to see what other team members are capable of, and a reason to reimagine how work gets done in the group.

By practicing PQ Reps daily, you can reduce the potency of your Saboteurs as you strengthen your mental fitness, improve the productivity of you and your team, and navigate challenges with greater ease.

Don't Be the Bad Boss

Perhaps you are one of the fortunate few who haven't the slightest idea what a bad boss looks like. So, how could you possibly see it in yourself? Well, to start, catch yourself and put a stop to it if you find you're behaving like one of these people we all hate to work for:

- **The Micromanager,** who delegates, but not really

- **The Dr. Jekyll and Mr. Hyde,** who leaves you guessing as to how they will react

- **The Credit Stealer,** who takes credit for your great ideas

- **The Public Berater,** who cuts you down in public when a quiet word in private would do

- **The Sphinx,** who never provides any feedback or teaches you anything

- **The "Too Nice" Boss,** who is a pushover but secretly resents things... and you wonder whether they will stand up for you when it counts

- **The Disorganized Boss,** who keeps you from getting things done and drops assignments on your desk at 5 p.m. on Fridays

*Sadly, this list is not exhaustive.

How to Become a Talent Magnet

Before we dive into the how-to of building a team that draws the smartest people in their respective areas, I'd like to dispel a myth.

We tend to think that if we have high retention rates, we have no talent issues. This is not the case. At the very least, your team will retire at some point—possibly all at once. At the worst, you may not be able to keep up with the changing times, which can deter fresh talent.

Take Will's finance team...

The new CEO had unveiled a strategic vision and plan that required bold new thinking, but finance was filled with skilled accountants and project managers who had spent the last 20 years maintaining the status quo.

As head of finance, Will needed to make a dramatic change in his team but struggled to field new candidates. Part of the issue was that there was too much job security (I know that sounds strange). People tended to join as juniors and work until they retired. They were in no way cutting-edge.

Then, there was Will. He was not a bold thinker or visionary. Will had made a name for himself as a "safe pair of hands" for the previous regime. He didn't know how to attract and nurture those who could do what the current CEO needed the group to do.

If someone had asked Will whether people wanted to work for his group, he would have said an emphatic yes. Just look at his retention rates! But that's not enough. You need (and your group needs) to be attractive to the broader organization, as well as in the external job market.

This is essential for three reasons:

First, you're increasingly competing for scarce high-quality talent. In your early management days, you pretty much had to work with whoever was assigned to you. Mid-career, however, you need to actively attract the best... because those skills you desperately need? Everyone else wants them too.

Second, how well you attract talent sends powerful signals upward. As one CEO I worked with put it bluntly, "I judge my VPs not by what they accomplish, but by who wants to work for them." The best talent flows to the best leaders, and senior executives know this. They're watching.

Third, the complexity of mid-career leadership demands a higher caliber team. You simply can't afford B-players in key positions anymore. Not if you want results that get noticed.

The performance gap between average and excellent talent widens dramatically at this level. So do the consequences of your hiring decisions. When you're able to attract more interest than you have seats, recruiting is far easier. You'll have a choice of people rather than having to settle for second best.

Rule 1: Let go when the time comes.

Teams and organizations need to have fresh eyes, ears, and energy. Stagnation is no good; there needs to be some level of flow. Which means (and this may be hard to swallow), part of your success as a team leader hinges on what your team members go on to do once they leave your team.

That being said, there are times when team members must leave—for the good of the company, as well as the individual. In such instances, we tend to think in terms of investment banking: up or out... and if out, you are escorted out of the building by security and asked to turn in your badge at the door. But there is another way to go about it.

The strategy consulting firm McKinsey is a good example. They have a history of treating their former employees as valued alumni. They do have an up or out policy, but those who "don't cut it" as consultants have been known to become corporate executives who then become clients of the firm.

My mother's enlightened view on parenting also applies: "Your children are not your possessions. You are their companion to help them grow and become independent." The same can be said of your team members.

Don't worry about trying to hold onto them at all costs or keep them from exploring options that are good for their careers. Those are short-term strategies that will backfire. Instead, keep the lines of communication open. Do your best to make sure people have a pathway to career success as they define it. If you're a magnet for talent, you will be able to fill your team with the best people for what you need at the time.

Rule 2: Give high performers what they crave.

Leaders who consistently attract exceptional talent have reputations for providing the things high performers crave, including:

- **Developing people who advance in their careers** Top talent wants to know that joining your team means growth, not just a paycheck. They're thinking three moves ahead.

- **Meaningful challenges that stretch capabilities** High performers run from boredom like the plague. They hunger for meaty problems that test their abilities.

- **Visibility and access to senior leadership** Talented professionals seek exposure where it matters. They want opportunities to showcase their work to decision-makers.

- **Ongoing learning opportunities** The best talent gravitates to leaders who invest in their growth daily, not just through occasional formal training.

People want to work for someone who makes them feel seen, heard, respected, and valued. They want to work for someone who inspires through words and deeds... someone who looks after their team members so they can focus on doing their best work... someone who is respected within the organization, who has the political capital and connections to get them paid, promoted, and recognized.

My skip-level boss, Xavier, was a great example. When he first joined the company to head the global department, we all thought we would be fired. Our previous head had not been effective in raising the team's performance, and we assumed it would be blamed on us. But a year later, we remained employed—and had collectively delivered record revenues and raised our rankings in the market share "league tables."

Xavier's leadership made the difference.

Xavier spent the first three months observing and getting to know each person in the department. He had a knack for knowing when to step in and mentor someone. He set clear expectations and established an inspiring common goal for revenues and market share. Every person in the department knew how they could contribute. He was present at all our team meetings and never failed to inspire us with his messages, even when we needed some "tough love," or when things weren't going well. He was transparent, and you always knew where you stood, whether it was good, bad, or ugly. He modeled the behavior and earned our trust.

The defining moment: after losing a big piece of business, for which he had personally been a part of pitching, he sent out a memo. In it, he detailed the lessons he learned and things he would do differently the next time. That was big. No one had *ever* done something like that before. We would have followed him anywhere after that.

As the saying goes, you're not a great leader if, when you turn around, there's no one following you. How about you— what's your reputation as a leader?

Rule 3: Create a team culture with a "cool factor".

What makes a group "cool" enough to attract top talent? It's rarely the work alone, though that matters. More often, it's the culture and leadership that make it stand out.

In my early days at Morgan Stanley, one of our most respected groups was the Secured Asset Financing Group (SAFG)—not exactly a sexy name. The work involved complex financial transactions to help businesses finance heavy equipment through leasing. Not the kind of thing that instantly attracts ambitious young bankers.

Yet this group became a sought-after place to work. Why? Because its leader, Hank, had created a distinctive culture characterized by three things:

1. **Intellectual challenge** Hank deliberately framed every project as a puzzle that required creative thinking, not just execution.

2. **Exceptional team dynamics** The group was known for its collaborative atmosphere, where junior members could speak up without fear, and senior members were genuinely invested in developing talent.

3. **Market leadership** They were pioneering new approaches that competitors couldn't match, creating a sense of pride in being part of something innovative.

These cultural elements created a group identity that transcended the technical nature of the work itself. People wanted to join not simply for what they'd be doing, but for who they would be working with and how they would be treated in the process.

You can create this kind of attractive culture in any group by focusing on what makes your team's approach distinctive and valuable to both the organization and the careers of the team members.

For example, what attracted me to the market coverage group was how entrepreneurial it was. Since the products were lower margin and there wasn't quite so much money at stake, even the junior analysts and associates were given the chance to work directly with clients and make an impact. It was the ideal training ground for building trusted client relationships early in a career.

In contrast, my peers in the M&A department were working on deals that showed up on the front page of the *Wall Street Journal*. That was their cool factor. But they were buried deep in their merger models and doing the bidding of three layers of managers above them.

When you create your distinctive culture and cultivate a "talent development engine"—a team environment that systematically grows people for bigger roles—senior leaders notice. It signals your readiness to join their ranks: you've developed organizational capacity beyond your immediate needs; identified and developed potential in others; built sustainable systems that don't rely on your personal involvement; created loyalty that extends beyond your direct team.

That's why leaders who consistently develop talent that succeeds elsewhere in the organization often find their careers accelerating as a result. Because senior leaders notice who builds bench strength not just for their team, but for the entire organization. They see who feeds the talent pipeline. And that's pretty cool, too.

Rule 4: Choose the right team.

Remember the days of gym class, where the teacher named two captains who then alternated in picking team members? Being small and more of a "good student" type, I was often one of the last to be chosen … until my classmates realized that I was sportier than I looked and a great cheerleader, so I was often on the winning team.

When it comes to work, you also need a winning team—and that means choosing the right people for the right roles. You want to put team members into roles where they can use their strengths and interests to achieve superior results.

Resist the instinct to hire in your likeness. That is, avoid the "mini-me" trap, where you're drawn to hire the people who remind you of a younger version of yourself. As one of my mentors explained, "I used to think it was best to have a team of very similar people because we could get things done faster. We came from the same schools, had similar backgrounds, and could practically finish each other's sentences. But then I realized we were only making incremental improvements while some competitors were leapfrogging us. Sure, we made decisions faster, but we weren't seeing all the options and opportunities because we all had the same blind spots."

From that point forward, he built his teams to include a variety of people and viewpoints. Their debates became richer, and they had more new ideas. The team's performance was stronger as a result.

While it's important to share a set of values, when everyone has the same views, the same background, and the same way of thinking, you get "groupthink," which ultimately leads to poor decision-making and subpar performance. It's far better to have a variety of voices and viewpoints around the table to keep the group robust, innovative, and heading in the right direction.

Lead Inherited Teams Well

You may be thinking, *This is all fine and good when you get to build your team, but what if I've inherited a team and don't have the flexibility to make changes right away?*

First off, you're not alone. Whether through reorganization, promotion, or changing roles, many mid-career leaders face the challenge of stepping in to lead established teams with existing dynamics, historical baggage, and varying capabilities.

This is precisely what happened to Rachel when she was promoted to the head of a division after her predecessor's abrupt departure. Rather than the exciting opportunity to build her dream team, she inherited a group with deeply entrenched habits, relationship tensions, and performance issues that had been allowed to fester.

"I feel like I've been handed someone else's problems to fix," she said. Half the team was resistant to any change, and the other half was waiting to see if she'd last longer than the previous two leaders.

So, yes, leading inherited teams requires a different approach than building one from scratch. There are a few hard and fast rules that will allow you to do this well.

1. Resist the urge to make immediate, dramatic changes.

Premature changes before you understand the existing dynamics often backfire. Just as my skip-level boss, Xavier, did, I take time to observe how people work together, identify the informal leaders, and understand the unwritten rules that govern team behavior. As Rachel discovered, what looked like resistance was often uncertainty about her expectations and leadership style.

2. Focus on establishing trust before driving performance.

One of my mentors has a saying, "slow is smooth, and smooth is fast." So, while it feels slower, taking the time to earn their confidence early on will make it easier to make significant changes later on. This starts with understanding each team member's strengths, aspirations, and concerns. Rachel scheduled individual meetings with everyone on her team during her first month, asking thoughtful questions and genuinely listening to their perspectives before making any substantial changes.

3. Address the team's history openly but constructively.

Acknowledge past challenges without dwelling on them or assigning blame. When Rachel finally gathered her team for a strategic planning session, she began by saying, "I recognize there's been uncertainty and change recently. I can't change what happened before, but I'm committed to working with all of you to build something we can be proud of going forward."

4. Strategically decide where continuity serves the team and where change is necessary.

Not everything needs to be different under your leadership. Rachel kept several successful processes intact while gradually implementing changes in the areas most critical to the division's strategic objectives.

Within eighteen months, Rachel's division was outperforming expectations, and senior leadership took notice of her ability to create positive change in a challenging situation—precisely the kind of leadership potential they were looking for when considering candidates for executive roles.

There is hope! By following these principles, you too can transform your inherited team from a source of stress to a career accelerator.

Relish the Benefits

From the perspective of your career advancement, your ability to build and maintain high-performing teams is perhaps the most visible sign that you have what it takes for senior leadership roles.

Remember, leadership is fundamentally about relationships. It's the connection between you and each person, and the dynamics you foster within the team. The technical expertise that got you to this point will continue to matter, but your ability to build and lead a thriving team will increasingly determine your career trajectory.

When your team consistently delivers exceptional results, develops new capabilities, and grows into leadership roles themselves, senior executives take note. They see someone who can scale their impact through others—precisely the quality needed at higher organizational levels. As one senior executive told me, "I can teach someone financial analysis or strategic planning, but I can't teach them how to inspire a team of talented people to accomplish what seemed impossible."

It's both an art and a science, requiring continuous learning and adaptation. By focusing on these fundamental areas and applying the guidelines discussed, you'll build the foundation for a high-performing team that delivers exceptional results. All the while, you'll develop the next generation of leaders—including yourself.

PERSONAL ACTION PLAN

1. **Refer to the "nightmare boss" list from this chapter. Which 2-3 tendencies are you most at risk of displaying when under stress?** Be honest—ask a trusted colleague or team member if you're unsure. Understanding your "saboteurs" is the first step to managing them.

2. **How would your current team members describe what it's like to work for you?** Consider each person individually: Do they feel psychologically safe? Do you treat them the way they want to be treated? Do they know where they stand with you? What evidence supports your assessment?

3. **Looking at your team's current performance and potential, who needs what kind of development?** Map each team member: Who's ready for stretch assignments? Who needs more feedback or mentoring? Who might be outgrowing their role? Where are your talent gaps?

4. **What would make talented people, specifically, want to join your team over other opportunities?** Think beyond the work itself—what's your "cool factor?" What reputation do you have as a leader? What growth opportunities can you offer? What makes your team culture distinctive?

5. **Based on your biggest opportunity for improvement from the questions above, what's one specific action you'll take this week to become a more magnetic leader?** Choose something concrete that addresses your highest-priority development area.

4

FROM INVISIBLE TO
INFLUENTIAL

The Communication Skills That Matter

When I was being recruited to return to Morgan Stanley after getting my MBA, I had the privilege of an audience with Dick Fisher, who was then the president of the firm.

Even though this was a "selling interview"—the firm selling me on them, not me selling myself as a candidate—I was nervous going up the elevator to the executive floor. I stepped out onto the thick carpet, and an assistant walked me past the mahogany furniture and oil paintings toward Dick's office.

Dick greeted me at the door, shook my hand, and asked me to come in. We sat in two chairs quite close together, our feet firmly planted on the Persian rug. While I'm sure there was no fireplace on the 52nd floor of 1251 Avenue of the Americas in New York City, I will always remember it as a "fireside chat."

He asked me to tell him about myself, my interests, and how he could help me make this decision. He listened intently and waited until he was sure I had finished before he spoke. He answered all my questions thoughtfully, sometimes leaning forward but always relaxed and open. He gave me the feeling we were on the same side of the table, trying to figure out what was genuinely best for me. He smiled and spoke like a wise mentor or respected friend of the family. When he finally asked if there was anything else I wanted to ask or discuss, I realized every question and concern had been addressed, and I felt that he understood me. I was ready to go. Stepping back into the corridor, I felt amazed that he had spent so much time with me. It felt like we had talked for hours. But when I looked at my watch, I saw that only twenty minutes had passed. I signed up that afternoon.

This was one of the most amazing one-to-one communications I have ever experienced in a work context. I had never felt so completely listened to, and by such a senior person who clearly would have had far more pressing matters than recruiting a new associate to join the firm. He never looked at his watch or his phone—not even once. It was as though I were the only other person in the entire world.

When you can communicate in a way that forms this kind of connection with others, you have a greater ability to influence outcomes and reach the goals you and your team are working toward. You can get their buy-in, keep them engaged, and have them go the extra mile if only to please you.

As author Maya Angelou once said, "I've learned that people will forget what you said, people will forget what you did, but people will never forget how you made them feel." Make sure you're memorable for the right thing.

Upgrade Your Communication Style

Leaders who excel at communicating in a way that connects with people and influences outcomes do three things that others do not:

1. They focus keenly on the audience.

Instead of talking at someone, they make the conversation two-way by asking questions and inviting the other person to do the same. This helps draw the other person out, which, in turn, helps the one facilitating the conversation because it offers valuable insight: what the person values, where and how that person thrives.

With that information, answers can be tailored to the situation. There's no off-the-shelf sales pitch, no recycled elevator talk, no one-way megaphone, or the rehashing of a message delivered countless times before.

When you can flex your style to suit the situation and those you're talking to, you will have the best chance of connecting with your audience and being understood.

2. Excellent communicators listen with an open mind.

They aren't simply waiting for an opening to restate their case more eloquently or to hammer on their points again. They're genuinely interested in what others are thinking and saying. This means listening with all their senses. They notice the body language and tone—what's not being said—to pick up on the actual message. They are also open to hearing the ideas and concepts the other person is bringing. They listen to understand and connect with the other person. It's not listening to judge or reject. There's no trying to prove you're right or, worse yet, that the other person is wrong.

So how do you become an open-minded listener? Here's my favorite way to go about it: First, take care of all your needs before your meeting, so that you can focus on the other person and your conversation without distractions. Think the basics: go to the bathroom; make sure you've eaten and are hydrated; take care of any urgent calls or emails.

Next, take a cleansing breath—breathe in deeply and breathe out slowly—all the while reminding yourself to be neutral. This is the equivalent of an astronaut entering the airlock between the space capsule and outer space. It's that intermediate space (no pun intended) where you can see multiple sides of the same issue calmly.

Once you're with the person, stay present and in the moment; give your full attention to what the other is saying. No multitasking or looking at devices. No distracting nervous habits like jiggling your leg or twirling your hair. Don't cross your arms or frown, which can be off-putting and discourage conversation. Instead, maintain eye contact and an open demeanor.

Think of it as active listening where you nod, make sounds that indicate you're listening, or repeat back what you've heard. It's the opposite of listening to respond, which is when someone is so busy trying to come up with what they're going to say next that they aren't listening at all, just waiting for their turn to jump back into doing the talking.

If you find yourself getting defensive as you're listening, don't worry. It's a natural human reaction. But as they say, you're not responsible for the first thought that comes into your head, but you *are* responsible for what you do with it. In this case, it's to go back to the cleansing breath and refocus on keeping your composure and getting back to that neutral place. You can't control what the other person says, but you can control how you respond. It's not about you, and while it's easier said than done, remember that you don't need to take anything personally.

Feeling listened to and heard is a basic human need. By meeting this need through the quality of your listening, you will stand out simply because most people don't do it. You'll also be in a great position to influence outcomes, which is the mark of a great communicator.

3. They understand and draw on their sources of influence.

Whether it's based on thought leadership, expertise, passion, resources, connections, financial clout, or otherwise, they're aware of the strengths they bring to the situation and weave them into their narrative.

For example, Dick had his dedicated executive assistant prepare a briefing package ahead of our meeting and held all calls so there would be no interruptions. This was essential for him to be ready ahead of time and calm and composed during our meeting. He drew on his network of connections when he mentioned who he could put me in touch with. He conveyed his passion for the firm in his answers to my questions. The setting conveyed the power and status he had in the industry without his having to say a word: photos with visiting dignitaries; Lucites displaying the most prominent deals he had been involved in; accolades in the framed *Wall Street Journal* article on the wall next to the bookshelf. Everything about the way he communicated through his words, actions, and the way he showed up was consistent and authentic. I felt like I could trust him as a person. The total experience of how he communicated was what influenced my decision, not just the words. In fact, he didn't have to say that much.

Being a great communicator is a "linchpin" capability that helps you excel at many other skills needed for success. For example, being able to communicate powerfully will help you develop your presence and profile (which will come up in Chapter 9) and be seen as a leader.

Powerfully doesn't mean standing on a soapbox and making pronouncements or being the loudest in the room. Powerful communication is measured in the eyes of your audience. It's about the impact you're having on your listener, the connection you make with your conversation partner.

Be Smart with Your Conversations

Knowing how to communicate your ideas helps you get buy-in for the initiatives you lead so you can create new business and expand the set of opportunities available to the organization (see Chapter 5). Being able to have effective conversations is at the core of negotiating for what you want, building relationships, and managing stakeholders at every level—with your managers, colleagues, juniors, and external stakeholders alike, which we talked about in Chapter 2.

Joan is a good example. When she came in with the news that she was pregnant, I was torn. Happy for her, of course, but worried about the business implications. With a six-month paid maternity leave policy in the UK, it could make a significant impact on our revenue opportunities to have an experienced superstar like Joan away from her client base for that long. Just as my mind started racing with scenarios, Joan told me about her proposal.

"In your shoes, I would be worried about being away for six months. Instead, I'd like to suggest something novel. I would like to take one month of full-time maternity leave and then take the remaining five months on a part-time basis, spread over ten months. This means I'll be able to keep in touch with my clients and do business while also being around my baby for a longer period. I think it could be a win-win. What do you think of such an arrangement?" It was as though she read my mind.

With HR's approval, I was more than happy to say yes. Joan's creative proposal and the way she communicated it not only got her what she wanted—a more extended period with her baby while also keeping up her client relationships—it also improved her relationship with me.

Author and CEO coach Judith Glaser calls it *Conversational Intelligence®*, the ability to connect, engage, and navigate with others through conversations that build trust and openness, not fear and defensiveness.[6]

Glaser asks you to visualize where you and your audience are in a conversation, ranging from fear-based, protective, and closed off on one end of the spectrum to trust-based, open, and co-creative on the other end. The idea isn't to be perfect, but to be aware enough to shift the tone and direction when needed. For example, Joan's calm demeanor and innovative proposal helped me shift from fear-based protective mode ("How are we going to manage?") to trust-based mode, where we could co-create a solution that worked for everyone.

And if you sense someone's getting defensive, it's a cue to slow down, ask more questions, and reestablish safety and trust. I think back to how naturally Dick did this—he made me feel like we were figuring things out together, not that he was trying to sell me or win me over.

That's one of the key shifts to make when you're communicating with influence, moving from trying to *convince* people to trying to *connect* with them. When you focus on connection, you stop thinking of a conversation as a transaction and start treating it as a relationship. The words matter, but so do your presence, curiosity, and willingness to genuinely listen.

In my experience, the ability to create trust through conversation is one of the most underrated career superpowers. It can make or break deals, teams, and careers. Every conversation sends signals—either trust-building or trust-eroding. When people feel judged or dismissed, even subtly, they often shut down. But when they feel heard and respected, they open up. And that's when real collaboration and influence become possible.

Putting Communication and Influence into Practice

Great communicators are clear and engaging. They are effective at getting their point across in a way that others understand, whether in person or in writing....

One of the most notable is Oprah Winfrey. She has an amazing way of creating a personal connection with her guests and articulating her ideas in a way that resonates with her audience on a personal, emotional level. That's one of the reasons her interviewees feel so comfortable revealing their stories to her.

Winston Churchill is another example. He inspired resilience in the British people with his powerful, concise speeches as Prime Minister during World War II.

And let's not forget Dr. Martin Luther King, Jr., who continues to inspire and connect with people at an emotional level with his iconic "I have a dream" speech. He galvanized greater support for the U.S. civil rights movement.

This small sampling of great communicators not only got their ideas across clearly and powerfully, but they also inspired action, whether sharing their story, standing firm with courage, or joining a movement.

But you don't need to be on par with the greatest orators of all time to get your point across and influence others. So don't worry; you can develop this skill. Let's talk about how.

Understand Your Audience

Great communication is like throwing a ball to another person. You want to throw it so that the other person can catch it. How you do that will depend on who's on the other end. With a professional baseball player, you can throw the ball hard and fast; with a six-year-old, you'll probably opt for a gentle toss.

Similarly, you want to deliver a message that your listener or reader instantly "gets." To do that, you'll need to know your audience: who they are and where they're coming from; their level of interest and knowledge in the topic at hand; their likely perspective. You also want to try to gauge any objections they may have, if they're formal and polite, informal and hard-charging, or somewhere in between.

Some of the things you'll want to know about your audience are strategic. *What makes them tick, and what are their bigger aspirations? What matters to them? How do they win? What's their outlook on the world?* What you'd say to someone who cares most about the welfare of their team differs from what you'd say to someone who cares most about cutting costs.

Some of the things you'll want to know about your audience are tactical. *How do they prefer to communicate (in person, by phone, email, or text)? What's the best time of day for a conversation?* For example, my colleagues on the trading desk couldn't be "off the desk" for very long, so short conversations where I got straight to the point were most effective.

In addition to understanding these specifics, recognize that your audience will be listening with a WIIFM ("What's In It For Me?") mindset. No matter how generous or selfless people may seem, there's at least a part of them that's self-centered. It's human nature. So, part of getting and keeping their attention is to provide some kind of benefit or payoff for listening to and engaging with you. Otherwise, you won't be able to sustain their attention or get another opportunity to meet.

If you're attentive to this from the start, you're more likely to engage, connect, and influence.

When I was meeting with people at Arizona State University at the start of my senior advisor role, I knew it was easy to get the first meeting. Everyone was curious about this new person in the president's office. The true test of whether I had established my credibility, however, was whether they were willing to meet with me again. And that depended on the quality of our connection and the value they gained from spending those precious minutes of their lives with me.

People find value and connection in many ways. It may be learning a new technique or the good feeling that arises from mentoring a colleague. Maybe it's the opportunity to partner on a revenue-generating project or gain visibility with senior management. It may simply be how they feel after speaking with you. We all know those people who emit a positive energy whenever they walk into a room—they're "a breath of fresh air" or "a ray of sunshine." Others, on the other hand, walk around as though they have a dark thundercloud over their head, bringing down the mood.

By taking time to understand your audience, you can tailor your message and adapt your tone and style based on their needs and interests, which brings us to the second step.

Prepare and Deliver the Core Message

Early on in my career, my boss asked me to invite a colleague to join our upcoming client meeting. "Tell John it's a 'no prep meeting.' He can just come and talk off the cuff. He's good at that." When I dutifully relayed the message to John, he laughed and said, "I'm happy to join you, but there's no such thing as a no-prep meeting! How do you think I talk off the cuff?"

Ever since then, I've made it a point to prepare for meetings and even conversations that I care about, no matter how busy I am. It doesn't need to take long, but even a few minutes of preparation makes an infinite difference.

Follow these four steps to prepare yourself ahead of any important communication so you can deliver your message with impact:

Step 1. Define success.

Identify the one or two things you want to achieve before you leave the room or end the conversation. That way, you're more likely to achieve your purpose. Maybe you want to find out the answers to a few key questions or simply get another meeting. Other times, it may be getting a go/no-go decision or getting the okay to present a proposal. If you're working on your confidence with senior stakeholders, you may simply want to make your points without feeling nervous.

Having clarity on what success looks like will also mean you'll know when to stop talking once you've "made the sale." Even one word too many can ruin the entire conversation. Like the time we had just agreed on a fee with our client at the high end of our expectations. As we shook hands, my colleague said, "Thank you for your generosity." Few clients intend to be generous to their bankers. Our client left feeling they had gotten the worst end of the bargain, rather than both sides feeling they'd negotiated well.

Step 2. Set aside five minutes.

As someone who could grind with the best of them, I would work right up to the time I had to leave for a meeting. How else was I going to make a dent in my ever-growing to-do list? But that came at a cost. It meant I arrived flustered and often late, still thinking about the work I had been doing. Even though my body had arrived, I wasn't truly present for those crucial first minutes of the discussion. That made it even harder for me to contribute when I already found it challenging to speak up in meetings.

This is where the five-minute rule comes in. Instead of working right up to the end, set aside five minutes before you go into the meeting, call, or conversation to step back from the detail, clear your mind of competing issues, stresses, and deadlines, and remind yourself of the primary message(s) you want to convey.

When it comes to implementing the five-minute rule, treat it like a "pencils down" moment in a school exam. Set an alarm if you must, but give yourself the gift of those precious minutes (or longer if you can) to get in the right headspace. Just as the slight difference between 49% and 51% is vital in a "majority wins" vote, even five minutes of prep before stepping into a high-stakes situation can mean the difference between getting the result you want and coming out disappointed.

Step 3. Make three main points.

If you get the least bit fazed by how to organize your message, stress no more. All you need to do is synthesize your ideas into three main points. This "rule of three" is a proven way to package your message in a way that helps your audience follow what you're saying (or writing) and retain it.

Research suggests that the human brain cannot absorb more than three ideas at a time. So, even if you try to convey ten ideas, the cognitive overload you introduce means people probably won't remember any of them. At that point, it becomes like a grocery shopping list—there's no way to remember all the items unless you write them down.

There's plenty of evidence of the rule of three in everyday life: small, medium, and large; primary colors of red, yellow, and blue; Goldilocks and the *Three* Bears; a three-legged stool. And, according to my friends who've worked there, the global consulting firm McKinsey adopts this rule for presenting ideas on a slide deck—have either one bullet point or three, but not more.

If you find you have more than three points to make, challenge yourself to group them into three categories. The rest can be supporting points. It will be all the more powerful.

Step 4. Know how to make your delivery.

I've found there are generally two ends of the spectrum when it comes to people's preferences for receiving information. There's the "get to the point" type—those who want to hear the conclusion first (represented by the triangle on the left). Then there's the "give me the details" type—those who want to know all the background and details before you lead them to the conclusion (represented by the triangle on the right).

One type is not better than the other. But you do need to know which camp your audience falls into. In general, the more senior your audience, the more important it is to get straight to the point, or even start with the conclusion. If they want supporting points, they'll ask. This is especially true for businesspeople. Don't think that it's exciting to build up to a conclusion by starting with the details. People in senior leadership positions don't have the time or the patience to "wait for it…"

People who want background information first tend to be either in junior positions or academics. They're thirsty for knowledge and want to know how you came to the conclusion. They may also be skeptical of any statement that's not backed by research. In one of my first meetings with senior faculty members, I started with the executive summary, just like I would have done back in my investment banking days. I got such a barrage of challenging questions that I could barely keep my composure and not sound defensive. Just like those proofs in geometry class where you had to go through the entire logic before concluding the theorem was correct, academics are trained to be skeptical until you've shown the rigorous research that led to a conclusion. So, know your audience!

Step 5. Tell a story.

One of the most powerful ways to get your point across is to embed it into a narrative. In other words, tell a story. Storytelling is a part of our history as a species; it's how humans passed on knowledge before there was written language. When you're able to tap into this natural affinity for stories, you'll find your message lands so much more powerfully than any dry set of facts, figures, or data on their own.

For example, when I was interviewing for the grueling entry-level "financial analyst" role, people wanted to know whether I would be willing to dedicate the hours that the job demanded, even if it meant giving up practicing piano and the other hobbies on my résumé. Simply saying, "yes, of course," didn't seem to be convincing because the question came up again and again. What finally worked was sharing my back-story. Here's the answer that resonated with every interviewer: "I come from a long line of overachievers: my mother is a doc-tor and one of only a handful of women in her medical school class; my father is a prominent scientist in his field; one uncle was head of the central bank and another the minister of for-eign affairs in Taiwan; my grandfather was president of the Harvard equivalent in Taiwan; my great-grandfather was a judge in China. I have a lot to live up to." Finally, their heads would nod in recognition, and interviewers were able to check the box that I had the grit to do the job.

When you speak from your heart, you have the chance to enter the hearts of others, not simply their minds. And research shows that our heart and mind work together in deci-sion-making. Whether it's who to hire, what to prioritize, or any number of choices we face, our decisions are usually made emotionally, then justified with logic.[7]

So, what does storytelling look like in a professional setting?

You might employ a simplified version of the "hero's journey"—a story structure that follows a hero on their path to growth and change. This is useful when you're recommending something that the other person may not be expecting to hear or might even object to.

Here's how it goes: When we first started, we agreed to do X. Then, two months ago, we were faced with challenge Y. Based on the work we've done since then, we believe the solution is Z. In essence, you start with the situation as it was, then the challenge that's come up, and the solution you're proposing.

Another story model that may be useful is one I like to call "things have changed." This is useful when you need to get someone to change course without criticizing their past choices. You may even make them look good (just don't veer too far from the truth)!

It goes something like this: We've had tremendous success with X, and it has served us well over the years. It was the smart strategy then. However, things have changed. Now the smart strategy is Y.

Of course, even the most eloquently delivered message is ineffective if it doesn't land in the way you intended...

Create a Feedback Loop

The best communication isn't a one-way transmission; it's a dynamic exchange that relies on feedback to ensure your message lands as intended. Dick Fisher is a good example. When he met with me, he constantly gauged my reactions, asked questions, and adjusted his approach based on my responses.

This feedback loop is what transforms good communication into influential communication. Without it, you're essentially speaking into the void, like shouting across the Grand Canyon, hoping your message reaches its target but never knowing for sure if it did, or how it was received.

Thankfully, there are things you can do to ensure a feedback loop is at play, so your communications do not break down completely:

1. Watch for non-verbal cues.

Our longstanding client had just been hit with a hostile takeover bid by a corporate raider and needed us to fly out to their offices first thing in the morning to plan their defense strategy. My managing director had a conflict and arranged for me to accompany our senior-most takeover defense specialist, Charles, and the rest of his team.

When we arrived at the field meeting, the shock and stress on the faces of our clients was evident. It felt as though someone had died. Our team sat on one side of the boardroom table facing the CEO and his team. After a few handshakes and the briefest of introductions, the CEO kicked off the meeting by asking how we could save the company.

Charles began delivering his professional expert opinion. "Time is precious here, so I'll get to the point. Our team has done extensive analysis, and given your company's lack of takeover defense mechanisms, the best strategy would be to find a 'white knight' to buy the company. This is the only way to save the company from falling into the hands of the corporate raider who has threatened to break up the company and sell off its pieces."

The CEO's face turned red, and his expression changed from stunned to angry. Suddenly, I saw how Charles's expertise and experience were likely coming across as arrogant and superior from our client's perspective. His unfortunate habit of leaning his head back looked like he was talking down his nose at the CEO. His deadpan expression and delivery came across as cold and unfeeling to our clients, who were more "warm cup of coffee" types.

But Charles continued to lay out the facts for another five minutes, failing to notice the client's distress even though he was sitting directly opposite. As the most junior person in the room, I could see the train wreck happening but was powerless to stop it.

What Charles failed to understand was that our client was not ready to hear that they were defenseless, with the only option to find a more suitable acquirer. Charles's logical approach would have been a success with Mr. Spock from Star Trek, but these were nice people running a century-old company that still employed thousands of local workers who would potentially be out of jobs. They were counting on us—their trusted bankers—to help them put up the fight of their lives.

In the end, Charles was right; we fended off the hostile raider by bringing in a friendly "white knight" acquirer. But the way he handled the communication was disastrous. The client ended the meeting early and hired another banking firm to ensure they had the best defense. We were fortunate that my managing director was able to keep the client from kicking us out of the deal altogether.

All of this could have been avoided if Charles had been attuned to the non-verbal cues from our client and adjusted his communication instead of steamrolling ahead with his monologue. Here are a few non-verbal cues Charles should have picked up on:

- The CEO's reddening face and stiffening posture—classic signs of rising anger

- The exchanged glances between team members—indicating shared discomfort

- The gradual silence that falls over the client side of the table—often a sign that people have emotionally checked out

Charles wasn't lacking technical expertise. He was right about the white knight strategy. What he lacked was awareness of how his message was being received, which prevented him from adjusting his delivery to make it more palatable. He could have paused to acknowledge their concern, validated their emotional response to the situation, or asked, "How does this direction sound to you so far?" Any of these would have created a feedback loop that might have salvaged the meeting.

What's not said can be as important as what is said. For example, if they're crossing their arms, it may indicate they are feeling defensive; if they're frowning, they may be "voicing" their disagreement. In the case of the executive I worked for back in the day, if he started flipping through the pages of your presentation, it meant he was losing patience, and you had about 30 seconds left to make your point. These are all clues and cues you can use to modify your approach midstream.

As you watch for non-verbal cues in your conversations, there are a few things to keep in mind. To start, the implications of body language can differ depending on the culture and setting. For example, eye contact is a sign that someone is engaged and paying attention in Western societies, but it is considered aggressive and impolite in Asian cultures. Nodding can indicate agreement in some settings, but in others, it may be just a sign that they're listening.

Once you develop the habit of noticing what's not being said, you can begin to actively create opportunities for verbal feedback. This moves you from being a passive observer of reactions to actively soliciting input that can guide your communication.

2. Check for understanding.

Whether you're delivering a presentation, having a one-on-one conversation, or writing an important email, creating deliberate checkpoints for feedback is crucial. These checkpoints serve three purposes: They confirm whether your audience has understood your message as intended; they signal that you value the other person's perspective; and they provide opportunities to course correct before misunderstandings take root.

Here are specific ways to create these checkpoints in different communication contexts:

When you're the speaker:

- "Let me pause here for any questions."
- "How is this landing with you?"
- "I'm aware I've done a lot of the talking here and want to give you a chance to share your thoughts..."

When you're the listener:

- "Let me check that I've understood; [summarize what you heard]."
- "It sounds like X, Y, Z... is that right?"
- "So, where are we on this from your perspective?"

In negotiation contexts:

- "It seems like we agree on X and Y, but still have different views on Z. Is that how you see it?"

- "Before we move on, I'd like to make sure we're aligned on what we've discussed so far…"

- "How would you summarize where we are?"

Inviting input from the person you're talking to is vital to maintaining a feedback loop. I learned this the hard way in a client meeting where I had rehearsed my script to the point of memorization. Once I started talking, it was like someone hit play on the recording, and I didn't stop until I had finished the entire message. What can I say? I was nervous. Finally, a colleague interrupted and got the meeting back on track. Looking back, I should have caught myself in the act and paused to see how the message was landing for my client ("Before I continue, I'd like to check whether we're on track").

This check-in is equally important whether giving or receiving feedback, formally or informally. As the feedback giver, you need to make sure the person understands what you've said so they can use it to improve. That's when asking them to share what they've heard is useful. As the feedback receiver, you should ask for examples or clarification.

If you can get in the habit of checking in along the way, your communications will land in the best possible way, influence outcomes in the direction you want, and you'll be more effective.

3. Listen with an open mind.

When it's others' turn to answer, you must remain open to receiving what they're conveying, whether or not you agree. One of the biggest mistakes people make is focusing on the need to convince the other person that you're right.

First of all, no one likes to be "convinced" by someone else. We all prefer to come to our own conclusions. Second, this kind of mindset leads to becoming wedded to your position to the point where you start feeling defensive. At that point, it's hard to have a constructive conversation, but easy to fall into an argument that damages your relationships while ensuring you don't get the result you want.

It's a lesson I learned during a complex client negotiation. When the client pushed back hard on our proposed fee structure, my first instinct was to defend our pricing and explain why it was justified. But I caught myself before responding, took a deep breath, and instead asked, "Can you help me understand your concerns about the fee structure?"

What followed was a fifteen-minute conversation that revealed the client wasn't concerned about the total amount but about the timing of payments—they needed to spread costs across two fiscal years for budgetary reasons. Had I jumped straight into defense mode, I would have missed the real issue and possibly lost the deal. By listening with genuine curiosity, we found a simple solution that worked for everyone.

This is where the Conversational Intelligence® concept of staying in trust mode, where you can think clearly, is essential. When you can remain calm, cool-headed, and rational even when someone disagrees with you, you will have a tremendous advantage. Remember, feedback is a gift. It gives you a window into how others are looking at things, where you are shooting yourself in the foot, and how you might shift your approach so it will land in the way you want it to.

The feedback loop is what transforms your communication from conveying information into a dynamic exchange that builds understanding and trust. When you master all three elements—watching for non-verbal cues, actively checking for understanding, and listening with an open mind—you create a virtuous cycle of continuous improvement to become a truly influential communicator. Each conversation becomes more than an opportunity to convey your message but a chance to refine how you communicate in the future. This is how the best communicators (like Dick Fisher) develop their seemingly effortless ability to connect and influence.

Putting It All Together: Your Path to Communication Excellence

Remember, communication excellence is not an overnight transformation. It's built through consistent practice. Every meeting, presentation, or conversation is an opportunity to sharpen your skills. The beauty of this approach is that better communication leads to better relationships, and better relationships create more opportunities to communicate your ideas and influence outcomes that matter to you and your organization. So, whether you're making a case for a new initiative, leading your team through change, or positioning yourself for your next career move, these principles will serve as your guide to getting your point across and influencing others—without having to change who you are at your core.

PERSONAL ACTION PLAN

1. Looking at your upcoming week, which 3-4 conversations or meetings (both routine and high-stakes) offer the best opportunities to practice and demonstrate strong communication skills? Consider: Which interactions could build trust, showcase your thinking, or strengthen important relationships if you approached them more intentionally?

2. For each of these communication opportunities, who is your audience and what's their WIIFM ("What's In It For Me")? Consider: What do they care about most? How do they prefer to receive information (details first versus conclusion first)? What objections might they have? What would make them want to engage with you again?

3. Using the "Rule of 3" framework, what are the three main points you need to convey in your most important upcoming conversation? Practice distilling your message down to three clear, memorable points that directly address your audience's interests and concerns.

4. To what extent do you create effective feedback loops in your important conversations? Reflect on areas like watching for non-verbal cues and adjusting accordingly, checking for understanding along the way, and listening with an open mind when others respond, versus just waiting for your turn to talk.

5. What's one specific communication habit you'll implement this week to build trust and influence? This could be anything from the chapter that resonated with you (better preparation, active listening techniques, storytelling, managing your energy before conversations, or something else entirely).

PART 2

WORKING ON THE
BUSINESS

5

BEYOND YOUR JOB DESCRIPTION

Spotting Strategic Opportunities

"What would you do if you were running the firm?" asked the facilitator at the front of the room.

Everyone else in my breakout group was furiously writing ideas on yellow sticky notes, one idea per note as instructed. I marveled as my colleagues whipped off Post-it after Post-it, slapping them on the table as they went. All I could do was sit there like a proverbial deer in headlights, struggling to think beyond my little corner of the business. Ask me anything about my clients or the ins and outs of bringing in corporate bond deals, and I'd be able to give you chapter and verse. But I'd never once thought about the opportunities and challenges facing the firm as a whole. Looking around the room, it seemed I was the only one without opinions on the overarching vision and strategy.

That was the moment I realized I needed to seriously up my game if I wanted to keep rising in the company. My default strategy of keeping my head down, grinding away, and staying focused on the day-to-day of my role was now a liability. If word got out that I was so stuck in the minutiae of daily tasks that I had no idea of what was going on outside my silo, I would be dismissed as a worker bee. My peers would see me as someone they could outmaneuver easily. Worse yet, decision-makers would see me as lacking the ambition and ability to rise further in the firm—something I desperately wanted. But how was I ever going to leap from thinking and behaving tactically to becoming a strategic leader with vision? (Ironically, the corporate strategy team would one day report to me when I became COO for Europe, but that's another story for later.)

Somewhere in the middle of your career, developing a vision and thinking strategically becomes an essential capability. It's as if there's a big sifter that sorts those with leadership potential from those who simply perform well in their current jobs, promoting the former at the expense of the latter. No one will ring a bell to alert you. You must take the initiative to be ready when the time comes.

London Business School Professor Herminia Ibarra refers to this capability as "envisioning"—the ability to recognize new opportunities and trends in the environment and develop a new strategic direction for an enterprise. It's what I did 18 months before 11 European currencies became a single currency called the euro. My role was to envision the impact it would have on European capital markets, then come up with a strategy for positioning the firm and its clients to take advantage of it. Devising and executing on that strategy created a multimillion-dollar business for the firm and led to my transfer to London.

It's what I refer to as being good at "vision and strategy." You'll hear these words a lot from here on out. Here's my definition: vision is your aspiration for your business and your self—seeing what you *could* be in the future and what it would look like to win (however you define winning); strategy is the way you're going to get from here to there at a relatively high level—it's the game plan for winning.

For example, when we started the corporate bond origination business in London, our vision was to be the best corporate bond house as measured by our client relationships, quality of advice, and market share. Our strategy was to collaborate with our colleagues in corporate finance to target companies where the firm already had strong relationships and to offer superior advice based on our track record in other markets.

To make this happen, we needed to envision ourselves beyond our business unit silo and become the connecting bridge across multiple groups within the firm. We determined that we needed to go on an internal "roadshow" to share with each group the message about this new opportunity, what role each of us would play if we were going to win, and why it was a good thing for each colleague to embrace.

Don't Think You Need to Worry About This Yet?

You might be thinking, "How am I supposed to develop a new strategic direction when I'm in the mid-level trenches making the place run, with layers of top executives above me running the place? Isn't this *their* job?"

The short answer: no matter where you are in the food chain, you're not off the hook. If you want any hope of getting promoted to more senior positions, you need to demonstrate that you can think like someone in a more senior position. And that means being able to envision a winning future and devise a strategy for turning that vision into a reality. The good news: you don't have to jump straight to CEO-level strategic thinking and vision, just upgrade it a notch or three.

Being good at vision and strategy looks different at each stage of your career …

In the early years, it's showing you understand the bigger picture of how your work fits in with the rest of the organization. Take Calvin, my analyst, for example. He was working on a presentation deck for the following week's meeting with a prospective client. On Friday morning, he rushed over to my desk to say, "I just saw the announcement about that prospect being acquired. We should stop working on that pitch and make sure the mergers and acquisitions group knows about this, right?" Not only was Calvin right, but he also saved me from embarrassment because I hadn't seen the announcement yet. Why sink time and energy into a pitch deck if we no longer needed to pitch? That's what my boss would have demanded to know.

As you progress, vision and strategy involve spotting the internal and external factors that will affect the results of your unit and the organization overall. It might be recognizing that your sales team has exceptional relationships that you might leverage to introduce the new products in your pipeline. It might be noticing that top management has shifted their focus to growing the electronic trading business, which could affect investment decisions for your department.

It might include seeing broader trends in technology and understanding how these trends might affect supply and demand for your company's products and services.

Or connecting the dots between what's going on in another sector and seeing how you can adopt the same approach in your industry. It might include taking a page from the film industry and using flexible teams—where people come together across multiple functions on a project basis, and teams morph according to need.

Ultimately, it's about developing an informed view of what you would do if you were running the department, division, or even the entire organization. And with every step you advance in your career, you'll have more resources to inform your strategic thinking and vision. Each role you take on allows you to meet new people, experience different situations, and expand your network.

If you make it a priority to lift your head from the day-to-day grind, you'll travel in increasingly lofty circles. You'll not only rub elbows with new potential stakeholders, but you'll also have far more access to insightful ideas and informed opinions. These provide raw materials to hone your vision and data points with which to connect the dots so you can guide the future direction of the business and transform cutting-edge ideas into reality.

But we're getting ahead of ourselves here. Let's come back to you and your situation and the practical steps you can take to develop your vision and strategy skills, especially when your potential is not yet visible.

The Forces Holding You Back

Despite their best intentions to be more visionary and strategic, many of my clients have their fair share of forces working against them. They're busy with urgent tasks, tied up in back-to-back meetings, constantly interrupted, and pulled into firefighting mode. None of these is conducive to thinking broadly about future trends and how to take advantage of them. Maybe this happens to you, too?

On top of that, their success to date has been based on knowing the detailed facts, being the technical expert, and getting things done—all of which use different "muscles" than vision and strategy. Not to mention, it's hard to resist going after the dopamine hit of immediate gratification, the kind one gets from accomplishing something tangible. *Kudos for closing that important deal! Well done for finishing that big project!* Thinking and strategizing beyond your sense of clarity and accomplishment is the stuff of delayed gratification, which gets a score of 2 out of 10 in the excitement department.

But the payoff for building your strategic thinking and visioning capabilities is huge. When you have an inspiring vision and a credible strategy for achieving it, you attract resources to your cause—people, finances, and other assets. This, in turn, increases your likelihood of success. As a result, you get more opportunities to be recognized, promoted, and rewarded financially. It's a virtuous cycle, with each step building forward momentum in an upward spiral toward greater success.

Suddenly, finishing up the big project doesn't sound nearly as gratifying, does it?

The key is knowing you need to develop the vision and strategy "muscle" and investing the time and energy to get it done.

Even the Smartest People Can Miss the Moment

My former colleague Gina graduated at the top of her class from a top university. She was the one who caught all the errors before the finished product went out the door. She loved to make things perfect. Her attention to detail was exceptional, so much so that she couldn't help but catch typos even when reading novels and newspapers (those early years of training were hard to shake).

Add to that her efficiency, pragmatic approach, and willingness to roll up her sleeves and "do the work," and it's no wonder she was everyone's top choice to take on the most complex transactions. She was an amazing resource for the organization. Until she wasn't.

Looking back, Gina realized that there was a point when she kept doing the work on increasingly complex deals and focusing on the details of execution when she shouldn't have. She was simply too focused on the task at hand.

What had seemed like unnecessary "blue sky" thinking and discussion to a doer like Gina was actually her former peers demonstrating their ability to envision the future direction of the business and pressure-testing their ideas. They were seen as leaders and given increasingly large parts of the business to run while Gina languished as a "safe pair of hands" in executing transactions.

Even more galling was the fact that Tony had been promoted ahead of her. Back in the day, Gina had joked about her mentee Tony's lack of attention to detail and tendency to appear a little lazy, and she wondered if he would make it through the early years. But his big-picture thinking and instinct for hanging back to reflect before diving into a project were paying dividends.

How could someone with Gina's abilities miss the forest for the trees? She wondered how she could recover. It felt like she had gone from "hero to zero" without any sign that it was happening until it was too late.

Putting Vision and Strategy into Practice

Unlike Gina, my colleague Harry (whom we met in the introduction) was especially good at big-picture thinking and envisioning. Even though he started a year later than I did, he was promoted ahead of me. Looking back, I can see it was because he was perceived as functioning at that next higher leadership level, which ticked the "potential" box. When senior managers needed input from our department to inform their decisions on firmwide policies or strategic negotiations, they could count on Harry to have a well-reasoned opinion. Not only did Harry have good ideas, but he could also communicate his point of view articulately and persuasively (harking back to the "linchpin" capability of communicating with influence from Chapter 4).

Harry's strategic approach carried over to the way he worked. He managed to be a top revenue generator without needing to stay late or work on weekends (like I did). The bankers and traders in the firm also respected him. So, when the opportunity to run the department came up, Harry was senior management's natural choice.

As this case illustrates, there are three additional aspects to vision and strategy:

1. **Insight:** Recognizing how your role (and that of your group) could evolve and contribute to the enterprise's future direction rather than staying in the comfort zone of maintaining the status quo.

2. **Communication:** Articulating this future direction to others (your team, colleagues, recruits, mentors, senior stakeholders) in a way that's powerful and energizing rather than keeping your thoughts to yourself.

3. **Application:** Taking a different approach to your work with the bigger picture in mind, instead of grinding away on tasks that keep you stuck in your current job.

In other words, it's not just envisioning where the business is going and how to get there; it's also understanding the implications for your role and unit, being able to share your ideas in a way that engages others, and applying your insights to the way you go about your current work. This is what Harry excelled at—and you can too, by taking the internal thinking you do and making it visible to those around you.

This is also an example of how the capabilities are interlinked. Your communication skills from Chapter 4 come into play in displaying your vision and strategy skills, and this helps you galvanize your team and colleagues to become an inspirational team leader, as outlined in Chapter 2. All of this contributes to your presence and profile, which we'll discuss in Chapter 9.

You may be wondering how you can do this and do it well, especially if you're not blessed with the vision and strategy skills that the Harrys of the world seem to be born with. More importantly, how can you develop your vision and strategy without making it a whole big project that you don't have time for?

How to Hone Your Vision and Strategy Capabilities

There are four ways to hone your capabilities so you can become more visionary and strategic without needing to take a considerable amount of time or go back and get an MBA:

1. Understand the space you're in.

We'll take a deeper dive into this aspect because it's more nuanced than the others and forms the foundation for developing your vision and strategy ...

Gary Dirks, my friend and colleague at Arizona State University and former president of BP Asia Pacific and BP China, introduced me to the concept of understanding the "space" or context in which your business operates. This was critical to his success as President of BP China, building the business from the ground up to $4 billion in revenue. For Gary, understanding the space meant becoming extraordinarily knowledgeable about the culture, hierarchy, players, boundaries, and degrees of freedom they had as a Western company operating in a changing landscape in China. It also included understanding what levers were at his disposal to make things happen.

When you're thinking about the "space" in which your business operates and where you and your group fit in, a good place to start is with the big trends and themes in your sector. Consider the following:

- **What are senior leaders focused on or talking about?** If you hear repeated references to digital transformation in town hall meetings or see customer experience projects being prioritized above all else, those are clues that these may be candidates for what's driving the industry, or at least your organization's position within it. Also, pay attention to what gets budget allocation, which metrics are tracked most closely, and what themes emerge in earnings calls or strategy presentations.

- **Who are the other players operating in the space, and what are their strategies?** To what extent are they competitors versus potential partners? Are any new players entering the space? You can bet that senior management is looking at the competitive landscape, sizing up how to respond or stay ahead of the pack. It's useful for you to start becoming aware of this, too. Consider both direct competitors and those who might disrupt your industry from adjacent sectors—think about how Netflix disrupted Blockbuster or how fintech startups challenged traditional banks.

- **Is your market growing, shrinking, or being redefined by disruptors the likes of Uber or Airbnb, by AI or other technologies?** This has an important impact on the relative attractiveness of the sector overall and how your unit or organization needs to position itself to be successful in the future. Look at both quantitative indicators (market size data, growth rates) and qualitative shifts (changing customer expectations, new business models, regulatory changes).

- **Are the industry dynamics becoming more complex or more commodity-like?** This is likely to have implications for your systems, processes, and profit margins. Complex industries typically offer higher margins but require more specialized skills and systems, while commodity-like industries compete primarily on price and operational efficiency.

2. Identify your key industry drivers.

Once you've gathered this information, your next step is translating these observations into two to three key drivers that truly determine success in your space. Remember, drivers vary significantly by industry. What matters in retail won't be the same as what matters in consulting or manufacturing.

If you're just starting to think strategically or if this feels challenging, don't worry. No one is born a strategic thinker, but fortunately, we can all develop this kind of thinking and awareness if we choose to focus on it. Here's where some examples might help.

Let's say you're *the regional marketing manager of a mid-sized athletic footwear company. After asking the questions above, you identify the following key trends:*

- **Senior leaders are obsessed with** "Direct-to-consumer growth" and "sustainability credentials."

- **Key competitors** Nike dominates with brand power, Allbirds leads on sustainability, and direct-to-consumer brands like Rothy's are growing fast.

- **Market dynamics** Traditional retail is declining. Consumers want both performance and environmental responsibility.

Based on these themes, your key drivers become:

- **Brand strength** (recognition and loyalty)
- **Sustainability integration** (materials, messaging, supply chain)

Or maybe you're the *operations director at a consulting firm specializing in digital transformation, and your* analysis reveals:

- **Senior focus** "AI capabilities" and "client retention in economic uncertainty."
- **Competitive landscape** Big firms (McKinsey, BCG) have resources, boutique firms are more agile, and new AI-native consultancies are emerging.
- **Market reality** Clients want proven results, not just flashy tech.

This leads to identifying these key drivers:

- **AI integration sophistication**
- **Client relationship depth** (repeat business, referrals)

Don't feel pressured to get it right the first time. Sometimes playing around with different options gives you the insights you need. And don't feel like you have to reinvent the wheel. You can always bounce ideas off mentors or colleagues who are already practiced at thinking strategically.

In short, think through each category and identify any forces that affect the way your unit does business. Those are potential drivers. Then, choose two or three that seem most important for your situation.

3. Create your competitive map.

Once you've identified a few drivers, create a visual map that shows where your company sits relative to its competition.

This is where you take those industry drivers and translate them into dimensions for mapping your competitive landscape. Choose two drivers to start and plot your organization (or business unit, if you're in a larger company) against others in your space.

You don't need to be precise in calculating where each competitor stands at this point; you're simply making a first cut. If you ended up with more than two drivers in the previous step, experiment with mapping another pair of drivers to see which provides the most valuable insights. Make this your own and have fun with it.

For the marketing manager example, your competitive map might look like this, based on the following:

- Your company: Mid-range brand recognition, modest sustainability efforts

- Competitor A: High brand recognition, low sustainability leadership

- Competitor B: Low brand recognition, high sustainability leadership

- Competitor C: High brand recognition, moderate sustainability efforts

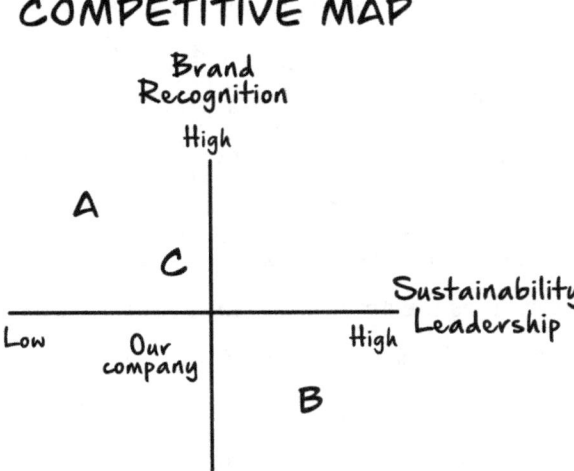

Once mapped out, it becomes clear your company is in the "low/low" quadrant of the graph, where it isn't differentiated along either of the key dimensions driving success in the industry. This means it's time to revisit the strategy. Do you go for sustainability leadership at the expense of brand recognition like Competitor B; take a more specialized niche approach and focus on branding like Competitor A; or try to take on both drivers to become the dominant player in the "high/high" quadrant?

As the operations director, you could plot AI capabilities against client relationship depth to see where the firm stands relative to competitors.

4. Understand your unit's role in the big picture.

Now, think about where your organization fits into that picture. Is your company a big player that dominates the market like Walmart, a specialized player that focuses on a high-end niche like Gucci, or something in between? Is your organization focused on manufacturing a product component like engine makers Pratt & Whitney and Rolls-Royce, or does it produce the entire product like aircraft makers Boeing and Airbus? Neither is intrinsically better than the other, but the answer determines the amount of clout your organization has, how nimble it can be, and what your organization needs to do to be successful.

For example, Walmart's scale means it has strong negotiating power over its suppliers, and its mass market pricing strategy means it needs to keep costs down. In contrast, luxury brand Gucci needs to focus on and invest in the cachet of its brand.

Finally, take a look at your group relative to the overall organization. What part does your unit play in the results of the organization—is it a core driver of revenues and profits, or is it a cost center that plays a supporting role? Is your unit the largest in the company, a small but mighty team, or something in between?

The goal is to develop a sense of the approximate scale and importance of your group relative to the overall organization, and the position your organization has in the overall market relative to other players. So, if you're working in supply chain at Walmart, you're in a critically important function due to the sheer scale of its operations and the emphasis on low prices. However, that same function at Gucci won't have the same importance as the groups that handle creative design and brand management.

Knowing the relative importance of your unit and its contribution to the overall organization will be helpful when you approach senior stakeholders. If your unit is the primary engine for growth or core to the brand, you're more likely to get the attention of senior managers than if it represents just five % of revenues.

Understanding where your business fits into the whole is also useful when you're negotiating or asking for resources. For example, there's a world of difference between asking for additional headcount for your team when you're in a rapidly growing part of the business or one that's highly profitable versus a cost center that management wants to keep deliberately lean. In the latter case, you'd be better off looking at ways to use technology to deliver what you do more efficiently.

5. Ask questions to generate insights.

The more senior you become, the broader your responsibility, and the less you can be the expert on any topic, which means it becomes more valuable to ask the right questions than to have all the answers.

When you ask questions, you have a chance to learn something new and have more "dots" to connect. And thinking strategically is all about zooming out to see a bigger part of the landscape, collecting information and ideas, and connecting the dots. This is the stuff of insight.

So, who do you ask and what do you ask them?

As for who, start with yourself. Prime the pump of your strategic thinking and vision, and ask yourself questions that expand your thinking beyond the day-to-day; get your brain to play around with "what if" scenarios.

The kinds of questions that generate the most useful ideas will, by definition, be open-ended questions where there is no correct answer. For example, *What if we stopped doing ABC? What if we had twice as much funding? What if we had ten times the funding?* (The idea of 10x thinking is a popular term in venture capital and entrepreneur circles. It refers to pushing yourself beyond incremental thinking into envisioning a bigger set of possibilities.) *What if the whole business went online? What would happen if we lost our biggest client? What would it take to become the best in the business, double our margins, or serve a new client base? Where are we at risk of having a new entrant disrupt our entire industry the way Uber did?*

Once you've primed your thinking, you can start having conversations with others. Choose people who are capable of big picture "blue sky" thinking. People from different parts of your organization, or even outside of your organization, can give you a different perspective. You might even choose to talk with your team to encourage them to think more strategically. You never know what ideas may bubble up (or where). You can also use AI tools to pressure test or expand your thinking. But always start with your thoughts to keep your brain sharp.

6. Reevaluate your current work with the bigger picture in mind.

Not all tasks or focus areas are created equal. This is the first rule of strategy. Gary Dirks used the concept of "Blue Chips vs. White Chips" at BP. It stems from poker, where the blue chips are worth a lot more than the white chips, and winning requires strategic knowledge of the worth of a poker hand and how much to bet. In a work context, the chips represent your time, energy, and attention, and the question is, how strategic are you in placing those chips?

As a perfectionist, my tendency has always been to do everything I take on to an exceptionally high standard without considering its value in terms of poker chips. Whether drafting the internal weekly update or a board presentation for a client, I gave it my full attention and worked on it until it was perfect, even if it meant staying up until two in the morning. This was often at the expense of more important matters, like getting enough sleep before the big presentation or carving out time to think. If my time were money, I would be guilty of irresponsible investment of funds. In fact, I would have blown through all my chips, not to mention the spare change at the bottom of my purse.

Learn from my mistakes. Demonstrate that you're strategic by spending your time, energy, and attention on things that matter. Recognize if you're dealing with a blue-chip issue or one that's just a white chip. How do you analyze the value of a task? Start by taking a step back so you can see the bigger picture. It's the power of a pause before diving into a task. In that pause, you can better see where the task in front of you stands in the bigger picture.

For example, how does the task contribute to the broader goals for your unit and the mission of the organization? Who cares about the issue or opportunity, and what difference will it make if you take it on? If it needs to be done, then to what standard and when? Who else could do this task? Who would love to do this task?

If there's someone better suited than you to take on a white chip task, why not let them do it so you can free yourself up to do something you enjoy or will learn from? In fact, a white chip task for you might be a blue chip task for someone else. For example, doing the pre-meeting research for the three hundredth time might be rote for you, while it's an opportunity to do something new and challenging for your new analyst.

This leads us to the hard part: let go of those white chip distractions that eat up your resources. It's tough to stop doing those tasks that make you feel productive, that you enjoy, and do well. For me, it's putting together spreadsheets (yes, I still love a spreadsheet even though I'm the CEO and have team members who are far more skilled at it than I am). But I've learned these tasks are akin to indulging in "comfort food." They may initially make you feel safe, secure, and cared for, but too much of it works against you.

This is where the concept of "Eliminate, Automate, Delegate" comes in handy. Popularized by Tim Ferriss in his book *The 4-Hour Workweek*, he famously stated, "Never automate something that can be eliminated, and never delegate something that can be automated."[8]

To put this into action, take a piece of paper (or a spreadsheet) and create four columns. In the first, list all the low-value, white chip tasks that you're currently doing but probably shouldn't be. Then, label the following three columns: Eliminate, Automate, and Delegate, respectively. Finally, go through each item on your list and put a check mark in the relevant column depending on whether it's something you can eliminate, automate, or delegate.

Another approach, especially for recovering perfectionists, is the concept of "good enough." This is especially useful for those white chip tasks you still have to do, but can't automate, delegate, or eliminate. Before you start doing those tasks, identify the standard required. What does "good enough" look like for this assignment? Having this boundary firmly in mind allows you to tell when you're veering beyond good enough territory so you can stop yourself from going too far.

7. Clear the decks so you have time to think and be strategic.

This may make me "Captain Obvious," as one of my daughters calls it, but I'm going to say it anyway: you must have time to think if you want to be good at vision and strategy. But if we all know this to be true, why do we struggle with it?

As with most things we put off, even though we know it's good for us, there must be some kind of payoff in doing what we've always done. For me, it's the satisfaction of checking things off my list. Embarrassingly, I've even added something to my to-do list after I've done it, just so I could check it off!

That means we need to focus on the payoff we'll get when we *do* make time to think. When you get to the top of a mountain where it's still and you're above the noise, you have a broader perspective and can see the entire landscape. That makes it easier to see things for what they are. It's more a state of being than doing. For achievers, it can feel scary not to be busy doing. But this is when you get good ideas. You don't need to do the thinking all the time, but you do need to do it some of the time. One of my colleagues approaches it this way: don the planning hat one day a month, the implementing hat the rest of the month. And stick to the plan. Don't second-guess.

What kind of cadence would work for you?

Devoting the mental energy to strategy requires a different kind of rhythm than "getting things done." As such, it can take 30 minutes just to get from task mode into thinking mode. That's why I recommend you carve out at least two hours (and get your assistant to hold this time as sacrosanct). Go to a different room or place where you won't be disturbed. Give yourself a real chance to think. That way, you can successfully oscillate between the big picture and the tasks required to make the big picture a reality. For a guide to conducting your strategic thinking session, see the resources section (www.thevisiblebook.com/resources).

When you think big picture and have a vision, it's easier to filter out those tasks and activities that cause you to feel unfulfilled and burnt out—stuck on the hamster wheel. When you hone these capabilities, you're no longer isolating yourself in a silo. You're seen as a strategic thinker, someone who has a valuable opinion, with a finger on the pulse, someone with upper management potential. That's what leadership is looking for.

The Strategic Advantage

Developing vision and strategy capabilities represents one of the most significant leaps you can make in your career trajectory. When you demonstrate the ability to think beyond your immediate role, spot emerging opportunities, and articulate a compelling future direction, you signal to senior leadership that you're ready for greater responsibility. This isn't just about having good ideas—it's about positioning yourself as someone who can see around corners, connect disparate pieces of information, and guide others toward a shared vision of success.

The mid-career professionals who master this capability become the ones that senior executives turn to for input on critical decisions, the ones who get tapped for stretch assignments, and ultimately, the ones who advance to senior leadership roles. In a world where tactical execution is increasingly automated, your ability to think strategically and envision new possibilities becomes your most valuable differentiator.

PERSONAL ACTION PLAN

1. **Looking at your current work, which tasks are "Blue Chips" (high strategic value) versus "White Chips" (low strategic value)?** List your major activities and honestly assess: Which ones contribute to broader organizational goals? Which ones could be eliminated, automated, or delegated to free up time for more strategic thinking?

2. **What are 2-3 key drivers that will determine success in your business sector over the next 2-3 years?** Consider: What are senior leaders repeatedly discussing? How is technology changing in your industry? What competitive or regulatory forces are emerging? Where do you stand relative to competitors on these dimensions?

3. **If someone were to ask you, "What would you do if you were running this department/division?" What would your answer be?** Practice articulating a vision and strategy at your level: What opportunities do you see? What would you prioritize? How would you position your unit for future success?

4. **How can you start demonstrating more strategic thinking in your current role?** Consider: Which meetings or conversations offer opportunities to share bigger-picture perspectives? How can you reframe your current projects to show their strategic value? What "what if" questions could you explore with your team or colleagues?

5. **What's one specific change you'll make this month to create time and space for strategic thinking?** This could be blocking 2 hours monthly for reflection, finding someone to discuss industry trends with, or applying "eliminate/automate/delegate" to clear white chip tasks from your schedule.

6

DECISIVE LEADERSHIP

The Confidence to Act When You Don't Have All the Answers

When my department head asked if I would go to London to start a new business for the firm, I thought he was kidding. Uprooting my husband and our three young children seemed outlandish, especially to do something I had never done before. Finally comfortable in the product head role I had taken on just eighteen months before, I was looking forward to a period of stability at work. Why would I throw it all away to move my young family three thousand miles across an ocean to an office where I knew almost no one to compete with every other bank for a slice of this new market? There were others in the department who were more experienced, knowledgeable, and strategic. Was I the expendable one they could risk sending on a mission that could very well fail? I didn't want my family to suffer and had worked too hard to gamble with my career. So, I said no.

That evening, I told my husband about the London opportunity and reassured him I would never disrupt the family, especially not for something risky. He couldn't believe I had said no to what he saw as a golden opportunity to step up in my career. He was on a sabbatical from teaching and coaching basketball anyway, and at the ages of seven, five, and one, the children would be fine. The family would relish the adventure, and being in a golf mecca would be amazing for him. "Go back and tell them you'll do it!"

It was easy for him to say, being the entrepreneurial one in the family. But my natural caution and a decade of banker training led me to see the opportunity as a huge risk. *What if the market never developed? What if the competition was so fierce that the business wasn't profitable? What if my counterparts at the other banks were better than me? What if I screwed it up?* At such an early stage, there could be no assurances, and I had no proven track record as a senior leader. Worse yet, I discovered Harry—my super plugged-in colleague from Chapter 5—had already turned down the opportunity; that meant I was second choice, at best.

My husband, on the other hand, said he would bet on me any day of the week. The high visibility of the role was a great opportunity to prove myself and make an impact. Wasn't I the one motivated by challenge? And this role would use one of my best strengths—bringing together disparate groups to achieve a common goal, which was far more important than being an expert in the markets where I saw myself lacking. Hadn't I been worried about the lack of future career opportunities with so many peers at or above my level in New York?

Looking at the downside of staying put helped reframe what felt like a huge career gamble into an opportunity worth exploring. Those conversations subsequently turned the opportunity into a calculated risk I was eager to take. If I had wavered any longer, I would have been left in New York competing with everyone else for a handful of leadership roles. That one decision to say yes changed the trajectory of my career and opened the door for opportunities I never envisioned, including becoming COO for Europe.

Demonstrating Your Decision-Making Potential Is Essential

This experience taught me something crucial about decision-making: the biggest obstacles to good decisions often aren't external factors but our internal barriers. My initial hesitation wasn't a lack of information; it was fear of the unknown and disrupting what felt comfortable. Yet as leaders rise in their careers, the ability to make decisions despite uncertainty becomes increasingly essential.

Decisions are, by nature, about risk. Your choices will either cost or gain you something, whether it's time, money, relationships, reputation, or something else of value. When you make a good decision, management is happy, and your reputation rises. When you make a bad decision, your reputation falls. No wonder decision-making feels hard. Committing yourself to a position or a path of action when you don't have all the information (and you rarely do) is risky business.

Ultimately, however, people who rise in their careers and become great leaders are those who can weigh the situation and make a measured decision. The more senior you get, the more you're expected to make tough decisions. On your way up, a great way to demonstrate you can make good decisions—even when they're not yet yours to make—is to come up with solutions, not just delegate the decision upwards.

According to the dictionary, a decision is "a conclusion or resolution reached after consideration," and decision-making is "the thought process of selecting a logical choice from the available options." Since a decision begins with consideration, a key ingredient is to have the information you need to come up with options and choose among them.

Acting Despite Uncertainty

On the one hand, there's plenty of information out there, even information overload, but it's not necessarily the right kind of information. From fake news to the usual half-baked, self-interested opinions from even well-meaning colleagues, it's hard to know what and who to trust. On the other hand, even if you have the right information, there are consequences to making the wrong choice. The wrong decision could make you look like a fool, lose money for the company, or even cost you your job.

What most people don't realize is that maintaining the status quo is a decision in disguise. Again, each decision carries risk. In fact, the "do nothing" strategy can be even riskier than changing the status quo. Just ask Eastman Kodak. They failed to make the switch to digital photography and ultimately went bankrupt.

So how do you know when you have enough information?

This is where U.S. General and former Secretary of State Colin Powell's 40/70 rule for decision-making comes in. He would only make a decision when he had 40% to 70% of the information. Less, and there wasn't enough intel; more, and it would be too late.[9]

Don't fall into the trap of analysis paralysis. Make the decision when you have at least 40% of the information but no more than 70%. Said another way, make the best decision you can with what you know in the time that you have.

Of course, once you've made your decision—thought it through, considered the information and the logic—you've got to act. The first part is necessary but insufficient. That's why I prefer Arizona State University Emeritus Professor Dan Brooks's definition of a decision: "An irrevocable allocation of resources."

Professor Brooks gives the example of saying, "I've decided to lose weight." In his view, that's at best a plan or an intention, and in many cases a hope or fantasy. It's definitely not a decision—until you act. Without action, no value is created. That's why decision-making must include action.

Decision-Making Traps That Can Hold You Back

Failing to make decisions and act despite uncertainty is typically due to falling into one (or both) of these two decision-making traps:

Trap 1: Analysis paralysis – the failure to decide

This trap is especially easy to fall into for high achievers who want to "get it right." But to keep advancing past middle management, you have to show you can make decisions crisply and cleanly without falling into the "analysis paralysis" trap.

Indecision puts the whole team on hold, and no forward progress is possible. To illustrate this point, if you're going back and forth between a detailed slide deck and a one-page agenda for the client meeting, your team cannot move forward until you make a decision, and then you have to scramble to meet the deadline.

It brings to mind the time we waited almost a year for management to decide how to share the credit between two units. The existing incentive structure caused the units to compete for the same client, which was inefficient and made us appear disjointed as a firm. But our proposed solution caused issues in other parts of the business. In the end, we ended up with the status quo and found a way to make it work, but not without a lot of disruption, wasted time, and energy as we jockeyed for position.

While taking time to analyze and reflect before making a tough decision is natural and even a good idea, give it a time limit. And don't show your hesitation in public, which is the equivalent of watching your eye doctor hover over her instruments before choosing which one to bring up to your eye. It doesn't inspire confidence, and it won't identify you as someone with leadership qualities.

Being indecisive ultimately cost me at least a year in promotion time. It had nothing to do with ability and everything to do with fear, perfectionism, and lack of clarity—all of which are the enemies of making and acting on good decisions.

Trap 2: The failure to commit to action

If you've ever announced a decision and then immediately wondered whether you made the right choice, you'll be familiar with this trap. Did you cover every angle? Have you thought through every scenario?

When you have doubts, it slows your progress. It's like driving with the handbrake on. Wavering once you've said "charge" causes those around you to become less committed as well. Lack of consistent execution can make a perfectly good plan fall to pieces. It can also drain your energy and reduce your ability to show up as the confident, capable professional senior stakeholders are looking for when choosing whom to promote.

Whatever role you play in the organization, your decisiveness (or lack thereof) can make or break your success as you become more and more senior. To quote American General George S. Patton, "A good plan violently executed now is better than a perfect plan executed next week."

This capability is about making strong, decisive choices and then confidently moving ahead despite uncertainty. You will come across as being decisive if you make the decision crisply, act on it, and move on. Get out of the habit of wavering and commit to learning from your choices instead.

Today, the world is so much more complex, volatile, fast-moving, and uncertain, which presents both challenges and opportunities to us as decision-makers. On the one hand, it can make us doubt our decisions. On the other hand, as things around us inevitably change, it gives us more opportunities to make adjustments (essentially, new decisions), much like a sailboat tacks toward its desired destination under changing wind and wave conditions.

The Path to Becoming a Decisive Leader

Now that you know the traps that can paralyze your decision-making, let's explore the key strategies for becoming the decisive decision-maker and action-taker you need to be. These strategies are designed to help you navigate uncertainty with confidence and demonstrate the kind of decisive leadership that gets noticed by senior management.

Rule 1: Make fewer, better decisions.

As Barry Schwartz writes about in *The Paradox of Choice*, the human brain can only make so many decisions in a day before "decision fatigue" sets in.[10] That's why it pays to make as many decisions as you can routine, to preserve your decision-making capability for the important ones. For example, lay out your clothes the night before and decide what you'll have for breakfast the following morning.

A big part of being a CEO is making good decisions. No doubt that's why many of them have their own routines. Steve Jobs always wore a black turtleneck and black pants. My friend and former CEO always orders the same lunch at a restaurant: Caesar salad with grilled chicken.

What decisions can you make routine so you can focus on what matters most?

Rule 2: Choose your decision timing strategically.

According to Schwartz, the best time of day for decision-making is in the morning before you've used up your quota. This is especially true for the decisions that are challenging because of their complexity and impact. That's why I like to do the big, important tasks first thing in the morning.

In a work context, this could be planning out an important marketing campaign, preparing for a management presentation, or writing a client proposal. While these tasks may not sound like they require momentous decision-making, they do involve making a myriad of choices about what to include versus leave out, how to phrase the message, and the order in which to lay out your case so you get the best result. Dealing with these critical decisions requires clarity of thought, which you're more likely to have earlier in the day.

This reminds me of the book by Brian Tracy called *Eat That Frog*. Tracy suggests that if your job is to eat a frog, do it first thing so you aren't wasting energy dreading the awful task all day. And if your job is to eat two frogs, eat the bigger, uglier one first.[11]

What kinds of projects or tasks would be easier for you to tackle at the start of your day?

Rule 3: Frame decisions for success.

Decisions can be hard to make, and sometimes they come down to the way they're framed. That is, the way they're presented, thought about, or looked at. For example, if you frame a decision by looking at the downside or the risks (e.g., "We could lose as much as $100,000 with project X, but only $10,000 with project Y"), you will likely skew the choice to the more conservative option. On the other hand, if you present the upside opportunity, it usually leads to selecting the option with the bigger potential payoff.

The number of options you consider also comes into play. Evaluating a dozen possibilities is overwhelming, but if you whittle them down to three or four, it becomes much easier to make an intelligent choice. On the other hand, if there are just two options, you may well be limiting yourself or even creating a false dichotomy when there are more than two options. As they say, "One option is an option. Two options are a dilemma. Three (or more) options are a choice."

This is particularly important when you are faced with an unpleasant trade-off. In cases of "either/or" decisions, where neither option is attractive, challenge yourself to find the "third way." This is what former Dean of the Rotman School of Business, Roger Martin, introduces in his book *The Opposable Mind*—it's taking the best of both alternatives and creating a new, superior option.[12]

For example, we were asked to choose between two competing teams who both wanted to offer us a service—one more dependable, but the other one more creative. We reframed the decision to focus on how best to achieve our bigger goal of having a creative solution we could count on. This led us to challenge the "either/or" assumption and to ultimately ask the two teams to work together to provide us with the best of both worlds.

Rule 4: Establish your decision-making protocol.

Just as golfers have pre-shot routines, it's helpful to have pre-established ground rules for you and your team when it comes to making decisions. Clarify who makes which decisions; keep abreast of what's at stake for various stakeholders; and define whether, when, and how to consult others (or not). Figure out what works for you and create a routine.

An effective decision protocol doesn't need to be complicated. In fact, the simpler it is, the more likely you'll use it consistently. Here's a basic framework that has served me and many of my coaching clients well:

- **Define the decision clearly.** What exactly are you deciding? Be specific.

- **Establish your criteria.** What factors matter most in this decision?

- **Gather appropriate information.** Remember Powell's 40/70 rule.

- **Consult the right people.** Who has expertise or will be affected?

- **Make the decision.** Set a deadline and stick to it.

- **Communicate with clarity and confidence.** No hedging or apologizing.

- **Move forward decisively.** Once decided, commit fully to execution.

When I was considering the London opportunity, I unconsciously followed elements of this protocol. I defined what I was deciding (whether to uproot my family for a new role), established criteria (impact on family, career growth, likelihood of success), gathered information (discussed with my husband, talked to my mentors and selected colleagues—which was how I learned someone else had been offered the role!), consulted key stakeholders (my family and managers), made the decision (yes), communicated it (back to my department head), and moved forward decisively (embracing the opportunity fully).

Having a consistent approach to decisions builds your confidence and signals to colleagues and senior stakeholders that you can be trusted with bigger responsibilities. And when your team sees you approach decisions methodically rather than haphazardly, they gain confidence in your leadership.

Rule 5: Let values underpin your decisions.

Our decisions are based on our values. That's why it's so important to know what the values are at a variety of levels: your personal values, those of your team, and those of the organization.

At the personal level, you can identify your values by answering these questions:

- **What matters most to me?**

Your list might include things like continuously learning and growing, having a feeling of well-being, honoring your relationships with family, or leaving the planet in a better state than it is in today. Whatever is on your list, take a look at your day-to-day behavior and see whether these are showing up. If there's a misalignment, take an honest look at whether your list was more about what you think *should* be on your list of values, or if they're truly your values but you're not living them out. Both insights are helpful.

- **What do I feel passionately about so strongly that I will act on it even when it's unpopular?**

For me, it's fairness, and this shows up when I see someone being mistreated or made to feel small in a meeting. In those situations, I can't help but say something and give voice to those who may not have it. What might this be for you?

- **When have I been happiest and most proud of myself?**

Looking at your answers and observing the common themes across situations can give you clues as to what you value. For example, I'm happiest when learning something new and then passing on my knowledge to others so they can succeed more easily. This also ties to my values of learning and helping others.

- **What are the 3–5 best decisions I've made?**

  Understanding why those were good decisions and how you made them will also give you clues as to your values. Going back to my London decision, I can see the underlying value of courage coming through. I wonder what your best decisions reveal about your values?

There are several lists and self-assessments, like the VIA tool, that help you identify your top values. Don't worry about getting it absolutely right. It can take a while to home in on the top three to five values that are at the foundation of who you are. Just make a start, and then test them out as you make decisions going forward.

At the team level, it's helpful to have a conversation about what the team wants to adopt as its values. You can test these against what each person sees as their core values. If you discover there's a conflict, then talk about it. It's more important to recognize where there's a clash of values now than to wait until it shows up as a problem later.

Embedded in every organization is a "touchstone"—the single objective that matters most to the organization's success. It acts as a guiding principle in making difficult decisions. Sometimes it's clearly stated; other times, you have to figure it out yourself. But it's worth figuring out so that you can make sure you've joined an organization whose values align with your own. Again, this is something you can talk about with colleagues and managers. As we saw in Chapter 4, having this kind of common goal or mission is helpful not only to your decision-making but also for influencing others to get on board with what you're trying to accomplish.

When values guide your decisions, you create a consistent pattern of choices that builds trust with others. They begin to understand not just *what* you decide, but *why* you decide the way you do. This predictability is a hallmark of strong leadership and helps others follow you with confidence.

Putting Decision-Making into Practice

Now that we've explored the key principles for becoming a decisive leader, let's turn to how you can apply these in day-to-day settings, because you build your decision-making muscle in everyday situations ...

Rule 1: Tailor your approach to the decision type.

Not all decisions require the same approach. Here are five types of decision-making situations and strategies for how to approach each one:

- **High-Stakes Decisions** Decisions with significant consequences—like my London opportunity—require a more deliberate approach. These deserve your best thinking time, wider consultation, and careful consideration of alternatives. This is where to use your full decision protocol and ensure you've considered both the short- and long-term implications.

- **Reversible Decisions** These are the non-permanent decisions. If you try something and it doesn't work, you can return to your previous state or take a different approach without major repercussions. Jeff Bezos calls these "two-way door" decisions because you can back out if needed.[13] For example, choosing headlines to split-test in a marketing campaign, picking a collaboration tool for your team, or selecting a caterer for your offsite event. These types of decisions allow you to move faster, with less analysis. Give it your best shot, but don't over-invest. If you can easily reverse course, don't waste precious decision-making energy on overthinking.

- **Routine decisions** For decisions you make regularly, create systems, templates, or rules of thumb. This preserves your mental energy and creates consistency. For example, if your job involves reviewing vendor proposals or assessing hiring candidates, establish a standardized evaluation process.

- **Time-sensitive decisions** When the clock is ticking, focus on the must-have criteria rather than the nice-to-haves. Gather the most essential information, consult only the most critical stakeholders, and be ready to act quickly. Remember that in many cases, a good decision now is better than a perfect decision later.

- **Team decisions vs. individual decisions** Be clear about which decisions you'll make alone and which deserve team input. For decisions requiring buy-in or diverse perspectives, involve others appropriately. But don't abdicate your responsibility when a clear leadership decision is needed.

Rule 2: Build your decision-making muscle through practice.

Decision-making is a skill that improves with practice. Here are ways to strengthen this capability:

- **Start with smaller decisions.** Like any muscle, your decision-making ability gets stronger with regular exercise. Practice making smaller decisions quickly and confidently, then evaluate the outcomes to refine your approach. For me, it was choosing what to order from a menu (I used to agonize over what the perfect meal would be). What might these be for you?

- **Conduct post-decision reviews.** After important decisions, take time to reflect. What went well? What would you do differently next time? This reflection cycle accelerates your learning and improves future decisions. One of my mentors calls this the "went well, do differently" exercise, and he does this with his team after every project.

- **Find a decision-making mentor.** Is there someone whose decision-making you admire? Observe how they approach choices, what factors they consider, and how they communicate decisions to others. In an ideal world, you would discuss their decision-making methods with them. But even using them as a role model from afar is powerful. And finding the opposite—someone who isn't skilled at making decisions—can be useful as an example of what you *don't* want to do.

- **Create accountability.** Tell someone about your decision and your implementation plans. This external accountability increases the likelihood you'll follow through rather than continually second-guessing yourself. If you choose someone who can also give wise counsel, this can serve as a chance to bounce your ideas off of someone whose input you trust—a double benefit.

Decision-making can feel scary, especially when there's something at stake for you, your team, or your organization. But this is where the idea of "feel the fear and do it anyway" is essential. Your ability to make decisions crisply and decisively is not only crucial for advancing in the organization but also for making your journey enjoyable. When you hesitate, waver, or ruminate, it depletes mental energy, which in turn leads to burnout.

So, clear your decks to focus on the most critical decisions. Learn from each decision you make—good, bad, or neutral—and keep your values front and center. By following these princi-ples, you'll develop the decisive leadership that opens doors to greater opportunities and responsibilities in your career.

Bringing It All Together: From Hesitation to Decisive Action

Reflecting on my London decision, I realize it embodied all the elements of effective decision-making we've discussed in this chapter. Initially trapped in analysis paralysis, weighing end-less "what-ifs" that kept me from seeing the opportunity for what it was, my husband's perspective helped me reframe the decision from a risky gamble to a calculated risk worth taking. Once I committed, it was easier to move forward decisively, channeling my energy into making the most of the opportu-nity rather than second-guessing myself.

That pivotal decision transformed my career trajec-tory. More importantly, it taught me that the most signif-icant moments in our careers often come disguised as diffi-cult decisions made under uncertainty. Learning to navigate these moments with clarity and confidence is what separates those who advance to senior leadership from those who pla-teau mid-career. Maybe you can relate to this, too?

My decision to "go for it" became a defining characteristic of my leadership style. Senior leaders noticed and trusted me with increasingly complex responsibilities because they knew

I had good business judgment and wouldn't waver in the face of uncertainty or complexity. I built a reputation as someone who could assess situations quickly, make sound decisions, and execute with conviction.

This is the essence of what decision-making capability can do for your career. It's not simply about making the right call—though that's undoubtedly important. It's about demonstrating you can handle the weight of responsibility that comes with senior leadership. It's about showing that you can move an organization forward even when the path isn't obvious.

By applying the principles discussed—avoiding the traps of analysis paralysis and wavering, making fewer but better decisions, choosing your timing strategically, framing decisions effectively, establishing your protocols, and letting your values guide you—you'll build this essential capability.

The path to decisive leadership isn't about eliminating uncertainty or having perfect information. It's about having the wisdom to know when you have enough information and the courage to move forward. Most importantly, it's about learning and improving with each decision you make.

As my father told me when I was ruminating about a past decision that felt like a mistake, "Don't look back, look forward. That's why the eyes are in the front of the head." (By the way, I've learned more from my "bad" decisions than from all the "good" ones put together.)

Remember, decisive leadership, like any skill, strengthens with practice. Start with the smaller decisions in your current role. Apply the principles we've discussed. Notice what works and what doesn't. Reflect and adjust. Over time, you'll develop the decisive leadership that opens doors to greater opportunities.

So, the next time you face a difficult decision, remember my London story. Feel the fear, recognize the trap you might be falling into, apply your decision protocol, take action—and keep moving forward.

PERSONAL ACTION PLAN

1. **Reflecting on recent decisions, which trap do you most often fall into: analysis paralysis (struggling to decide) or wavering after the fact (second-guessing your choices)?** Think of specific examples. What triggers this pattern for you? How has it affected your reputation or results?

2. **What are your 3–5 core values, and how can you use them as a "touchstone" for difficult decisions?** Consider: When have you been happiest and most proud of your choices? What do you feel passionate enough about to take action even when it's unpopular? How do your values align with your organization's priorities?

3. **Looking at your upcoming decisions, which ones are "high-stakes" and deserve your full decision protocol, versus "reversible" ones where you can move faster?** For the high-stakes decisions: What information do you need? Whom should you consult? What's your deadline for deciding?

4. **What routine decisions can you systematize to preserve your mental energy for the important choices?** Consider: Daily scheduling, meeting preparation, vendor selection, or other recurring decisions. How can you create rules of thumb or templates for these?

5. **Who in your organization would benefit from seeing you demonstrate more decisive leadership, and what's one specific situation this month where you can practice this?** Think about stakeholders, team members, or senior leaders who need to see your decision-making capability in action.

7

CREATING VALUE

Transitioning from
Caretaker to Rainmaker

Wendy reviewed the stack of litigation files on her desk and realized she would need to request additional headcount if the caseload continued to increase at the pace of the last eighteen months. Not only were litigation costs rising, but so was the company's reputational risk. As an in-house lawyer at a Fortune 100 subsidiary, Wendy's job was to handle lawsuits once they came in. Like most mid-career professionals, she was excellent at her job. She meticulously prepared for each case, developed smart defensive strategies, and kept legal costs lower than her predecessors. She was a consummate caretaker, reliably managing her assigned responsibilities within established parameters. But Wendy sensed that to advance further, she needed to become what experienced corporate leaders call a "rainmaker"—someone who creates new value rather than simply maintaining existing systems and processes.

Caretaker vs. Rainmaker

Caretakers manage their existing responsibilities to a high standard. They do an excellent job at what they're assigned and solve problems as they arise.

Rainmakers create new value by:

- Expanding opportunities
- Enhancing performance
- Solving systemic problems
- Reducing organizational risks
- Creating strategic alignment

The transition between these mindsets is one of the most critical shifts for mid-career advancement.

When Wendy analyzed patterns across two years of litigation files, she discovered that the majority stemmed from mishandled customer complaints. Instead of simply processing the inevitable lawsuits, she started asking questions about whether these lawsuits could be prevented. She began to investigate the chain of events that led to these situations landing on her desk.

Wendy discovered that many situations could have been nipped in the bud before they became litigation events if people in the business units were more aware of two things: when to escalate issues internally, and how to defuse situations through better handling of complaints.

She developed an "Early Warning System" with clear triggers for escalation and cross-functional response teams. The results were dramatic: litigation filings dropped dramatically within a year, saving the company millions. Wendy won the CEO's innovation award and was promoted to head of litigation—not because she managed cases more efficiently, but because she fundamentally changed how the organization approached risk.

The essential difference between a caretaker and a rainmaker is this: caretakers efficiently manage existing responsibilities. Rainmakers create new value by expanding opportunities, enhancing performance, solving systemic problems, reducing risks, or creating strategic alignment. Both are valuable to an organization (we're all doing caretaker and rainmaker activities). But to keep advancing to higher levels, you'll need to operate as a rainmaker more and more of the time.

The transition from caretaker to rainmaker is one of the most critical shifts for mid-career professionals. It's not about working harder at what you're already doing, but working differently. It's not just the equivalent of handing in your homework assignment on time and in excellent shape, but producing outcomes beyond what currently exists, in a way that's tied to what matters most to your organization. So, let's take a closer look at what that looks like.

Welcome to the World of Rainmakers

You've probably heard the term "rainmaker" before—likely in the traditional context of a senior, silver-haired law firm partner who brings in the big deals and revenues that sustain the firm. Companies need money to thrive, much like a farmer's crop needs rain. So, in effect, rainmakers "make it rain" by bringing in the clients, deals, and money to support the growth and success of the rest of the organization.

For our purposes, I'm going to use the term rainmaker in a broader sense: a rainmaker is someone who makes great things—things that can be seen, felt, or heard—happen for the organization. Because every organization needs people who can make good things happen and deliver outsized results beyond what they've been instructed to do.

Having at least one eye (better yet, two) focused on the outcomes leaders within your organization care most about will allow you to grow your contribution and value most powerfully. It will help you make a bigger impact and advance in your career faster and more easily... without having to grind or sell your soul.

In the past, the senior law firm partners brought in the business, and everyone else focused on the execution. Now, even mid-level associates are expected to start showing signs of being able to develop client relationships and bring in business, or they don't get very far. Wherever you work, the same holds: adopting a rainmaker mindset and approach is essential if you want to demonstrate your potential to succeed at the next level of seniority.

You can be a rainmaker whether you're in a revenue-generating part of the organization or not. The concept even applies to organizations that aren't about making money, such as non-profits, governmental agencies, and educational institutions. What every organization needs to be successful are people who can be entrepreneurial and commercial in their approach, people who can create opportunity and success for the whole organization.

By having a "rainmaker" rather than "caretaker" mindset, you are more likely to be perceived as truly valuable at the next level and advance your career.

You Can Choose to Be a Rainmaker from Any Seat

Let's take a closer look at ways to be a rainmaker wherever you work and whatever your role. As we do, think about which would apply to you and your situation.

Strategy 1: Opportunity creation and expansion

The classical and most direct way to be a rainmaker is to grow the size of the business "pie" ("growing the pie," as I call it). Find new markets, clients, products, and services that add to the revenue of your organization, through identifying untapped needs within your existing client or customer base or creating entirely new revenue streams.

In my case, it started as just another weekly team meeting until one of our managing directors announced, "We're interested in exploring the business opportunities in the southeast region. Who wants to take this on?" My heart froze. There were only three of us mid-level team members, and I was the slightly more experienced one. I was used to coasting through the meeting in listen-only mode, but suddenly all eyes were on me and my two colleagues.

The ask was big, and I was scared as hell. Already busy working on assignments from my managing director, how would I find time to start meeting with companies in an area of the country I had never been to, or even figure out who I was supposed to meet with and what to say once I got there? I had no idea where to start, and cold calling sounded absolutely terrifying. It had all the hallmarks of something a quiet worker bee like me could fail at spectacularly.

On the other hand, I was the "eldest" of the three; maybe this was the equivalent of being the eldest in my family, where it was my duty to look out for my little sister. Was I expected to put my hand up and say yes? It would probably be a good experience to have, especially as I wanted to get promoted to managing director one day, and a key criterion was to be able to build client relationships and bring in business. It also occurred to me that there wasn't much downside for the firm, as we had never generated revenue or even talked to those prospects in the first place. That was probably why they were comfortable sending a mid-level associate to check it out.

And how would I feel if one of the others grabbed this opportunity first? I would have been distraught to miss out and see someone else grab the glory, if indeed there was any. In the end, my competitive nature, fear of missing out, and love of a challenge kicked in. I took the opportunity. As they say, feel the fear and do it anyway.

From developing a prospect list, setting up meetings, and creating a pitch book to renting a car, driving from company to company, and meeting with senior managers twice my age, taking the risk turned out to be a huge positive for my career.

When I got back from my cold calling trip, every one of the managing directors in the department couldn't wait to hear what I discovered. While my trip didn't make the company money, the outcome for me was instant respect.

As the biggest revenue producer in our department regaled me with stories of his own first cold-calling experience, I realized that taking on the challenge of bringing in business and walking in his shoes meant he saw something of his younger self in me. I now had something in common with the senior managing directors, and my reputation went from "one of the worker bees" to "one of the dudes."

If you're not in a direct client or customer-facing seat like I was, you can still find ways to adopt the rainmaker mindset of creating and expanding opportunity. Let's say you're in an internally facing function like IT or Operations and have developed a solution to a significant challenge in your organization. Consider whether other companies might have the same challenge; in which case, your solution could be packaged so that it can be offered to third parties. Amazon Web Services is one such example; it began as an internal function to address Amazon's own scaling and infrastructure needs and, by 2024, represented more than half of the company's operating income. At some point, someone thought like a rainmaker and realized that these capabilities could be monetized by offering them to third parties.

Now let's talk about how you might identify ways to create and expand revenue-generating opportunities from where you sit.

Questions to help identify your rainmaker opportunities:

1. What new markets is the organization considering entering, and how could you make inroads into that opportunity?

2. Is there customer demand for a product extension that you've noticed from customer feedback that would make sense for your organization to explore?

3. What segments of your target client base are underserved, and where is your organization well-positioned to provide the service?

4. Where are the high-growth segments of your market that your organization could succeed in but isn't fully taking advantage of currently?

5. What gaps are there in your company's product offerings that would be a good fit with the overall strategy?

6. What partnerships across departments could create new value for customers?

7. What internal solutions has your unit produced that could have relevance for other companies?

8. What new or emerging trends might open up new markets or product opportunities, and how could you capitalize on them?

Common Obstacle: Potentially being seen as going off on a tangent

The risk of going after a new market or product area is that instead of getting kudos, you're seen as veering into territory that doesn't fit with the company's overall strategy.

The way to address this concern is to have conversations with key stakeholders along the way to ensure you're not proceeding without support from management. This doesn't mean asking for permission; it just means broaching the idea with a few key people along the way to test your ideas, learn where the resistance lies, and make sure you're focusing in the right direction.

Be thoughtful about who you test ideas with because starting with a naysayer before you're ready can shut down a great idea before it has time to develop. That's why it's best to start with informal conversations with a couple of trusted allies first. This allows you to make sure you're not totally off base and to firm up your thinking before taking your concept to others.

Bouncing ideas off others will also allow you to start socializing the concept with people whose buy-in you'll need to carry out your plan. By observing their responses, you'll also learn how best to position and talk about your ideas to get the necessary implementation support. Once you have informal conversations, you can work on the more formal presentations to gather broad-based support.

Strategy 2: Efficiency and performance enhancement

This form of rainmaking involves streamlining existing systems or processes that save significant time or money, or both. Here, you're looking for persistent organizational challenges or friction points that limit success—then developing and implementing solutions that create significant new value.

Rather than finding your own workaround to problems (the caretaker approach), rainmakers in this category actively seek out organizational pain points—even those outside their immediate responsibility—and create solutions with broader application.

For example, as an IT manager, you notice that different departments are creating their own tracking systems for client interactions, which is resulting in duplicated effort and inconsistent data. Rather than simply maintaining the existing systems (caretaker), you could propose and lead the development of an integrated CRM solution that not only improves data quality but also enables cross-selling opportunities that can generate additional revenue.

Or maybe you're in human resources and see that the organization's lengthy hiring process is causing business units to lose top candidates, especially in technical roles. Instead of simply processing candidates more efficiently (caretaker), how could you redesign the entire hiring workflow, introduce pre-screening technology, and create a competitive assessment of market compensation to speed the process?

Or let's say you're in supply chain and notice that materials frequently arrive late to manufacturing facilities because purchasing decisions are made without considering transportation logistics. Instead of focusing on expediting shipments (caretaker), as a rainmaker, you could collaborate with colleagues to develop an integrated purchasing and logistics model that optimizes order timing and shipping methods.

Questions to help identify your rainmaker opportunities:

1. What recurring problems do you hear colleagues complaining about across meetings?

2. Where do you see the same issues arising repeatedly despite temporary fixes?

3. What obstacles, if removed, would significantly accelerate progress toward company goals?

4. Which inefficiencies or pain points affect multiple parts of the organization?

5. What problems have you personally developed workarounds for that could be solved more systematically?

6. What existing processes can be improved to deliver better results?

7. How could the current resource allocation be optimized to increase productivity?

8. What systems need upgrading in order to achieve higher quality outputs?

9. Are there best practices from one area that could be implemented in another to elevate performance standards?

Common Obstacle: Perceived overstepping

When you address problems beyond your direct responsibility, being seen as overstepping your boundaries or criticizing other departments is a genuine concern. But don't let that stop you. Instead, position your initiative as collaborative problem-solving rather than criticism.

Start by seeking to understand the perspectives of all stakeholders affected by the problem. Frame your approach in terms of shared organizational goals rather than departmental deficiencies. Invite key stakeholders to participate in developing the solution, which gives them meaningful ownership in the outcome. This approach not only defuses territorial concerns but often creates powerful allies in implementing your solution. And you'll be broadening your network of relationships in the process, which we'll talk more about in Chapter 10.

Strategy 3: Problem-solving and barrier removal

This rainmaking opportunity is about reducing or eliminating the barriers that hold your organization back from performing at its best. While the "efficiency and performance enhancement" element was about making existing systems and processes more efficient, this one is about improving effectiveness by removing obstacles to the company's success. This means identifying persistent organizational challenges—like conflicting goals or communication breakdowns between departments that cause delays in execution—and creating solutions that can be scaled across the organization.

For example, you notice two departments that are essential to a process have conflicting priorities and don't communicate well, and it's causing repeated project delays. A caretaker approach would be to flag the issue to your manager (delegating upward) and then continue doing your part of the process to the best of your ability. A rainmaker move would be to implement a cross-functional coordination protocol to resolve the underlying issues and therefore remove a persistent obstacle to meeting deadlines.

Questions to help identify your rainmaker opportunities:

1. What recurring problems are getting in the way of progress?

2. Where are there friction points between units that prevent the successful implementation of good ideas?

3. What roadblocks to success do people tend to complain about?

Common Obstacle: The level of authority needed

Often, removing barriers to longstanding problems requires a level of authority that's higher than yours. This is where you can exercise your creativity and resourcefulness to influence others. After all, when there's an ongoing challenge that keeps people from doing their jobs smoothly, you're likely to have a common goal to rally people around.

This is where your ability to communicate with influence (Chapter 4) and having a network of relationships (Chapter 10) will help you to move the initiative along to fruition.

Strategy 4: Risk mitigation and future proofing

Another type of rainmaker mindset is to anticipate and mitigate potential threats and prepare the organization for changing conditions. In times of rapid change, this type of rainmaker activity is key for safeguarding the institution while also strengthening the business's position to ensure success in any future scenario. While not directly focused on generating revenue, you are protecting the organization's ability to continue to generate revenue streams and positioning it to better serve its stakeholders.

For example, this may entail spotting potential threats on the horizon (e.g., new technologies, rising costs) and developing plans to address those threats before they become problems. Or, it may include anticipating the rise in a particular form of cybercrime and developing systems or partnerships with state-of-the-art providers to reduce organizational vulnerability.

It could be taking a set of compliance requirements and turning them into a competitive advantage. Let's say you're a data privacy officer in charge of implementing new data protection regulations (like GDPR), for example. The rainmaker move is to see it as an opportunity rather than treating it as merely a box-checking exercise to avoid fines.

First, you'd conduct a thorough analysis of not only what's legally required but also what customers increasingly value. In doing so, you discover that while competitors are doing the minimum to comply, there's growing market concern about data privacy. So, you develop a comprehensive privacy program that:

- Goes beyond compliance minimums to establish best-in-class data protection practices.

- Creates simple, user-friendly privacy controls that give customers unprecedented transparency.

- Trains customer service teams to confidently explain privacy practices as a selling point.

- Collaborates with the marketing team to position these enhanced privacy measures as a key differentiator.

In this case, rainmaker thinking means seeing requirements not as constraints but as opportunities to establish leadership and differentiation in areas that matter to customers.

Furthermore, notice how adopting this mindset can turn even a seemingly tedious or burdensome task into a business win, regardless of whether you're in a revenue-generating part of the business.

Questions to help identify your rainmaker opportunities:

1. Where are there constraints on the business that could be turned into opportunities in areas that matter to customers?

2. What trends and themes do you see on the horizon that could be challenging for the business, and how could you help set the company up for success?

3. What is the "golden goose" for the organization—the core revenue and profit-generating engine—and how can you help protect it from risk?

4. Where does the organization lack contingency plans for downside scenarios that could sink the company?

Common Obstacle: Being dismissed as overreacting

When you raise future risks or propose proactive changes to the status quo, some people may resist because they don't see an immediate problem. You risk being dismissed as overreacting or "crying wolf."

In my experience, the best way to overcome this is by framing your insights around a common goal—in this case, the critical outcomes that matter to leadership today and protecting those outcomes from downside risk.

Connecting your ideas to current business priorities will make the future risk tangible to decision-makers and colleagues.

For example, instead of warning vaguely about cybersecurity threats, you could highlight how a breach could damage the company's reputation and trust with customers—a top priority for the leadership team. You could also reference a high-profile case example from another company, which would be especially powerful if it were in your industry.

Linking future risks to current goals positions you not as an alarmist but as a prudent steward of the organization's success… and makes adoption of your rainmaker ideas more likely.

Strategy 5: Strategic alignment and integration

This category of rainmaking is about getting multiple parts of the organization to pull together in ways that multiply impact. Many times, teams or departments work hard toward their objectives but miss opportunities to contribute to larger organizational goals. Rainmakers recognize these gaps and bridge them.

For example, let's say you're a mid-level manager who notices that while your department is meeting all its key performance indicators, its work isn't fully supporting the company's new strategic direction toward sustainability. You could develop and implement a plan to integrate sustainability metrics into existing processes without disrupting current performance. As a result, your team's activities now directly support the company's strategic goals, and you forge important cross-functional ties with the sustainability office.

Or, let's say you're on a finance team and realize that operational budgeting timelines are not aligned with business planning cycles, leading to misaligned priorities. Rather than accept the dysfunction, you can think like a rainmaker and lead an effort to synchronize these timelines, improving efficiency and ensuring that financial resources support the company's strategic initiatives more effectively.

Questions to help identify your rainmaker opportunities:

1. Where are different groups unintentionally working at cross purposes?

2. Are there major initiatives where your team's contribution could be better aligned with the bigger picture?

3. How can you connect your group's work to what the executive team cares about most?

4. Where might collaboration across teams lead to better outcomes than isolated efforts?

Common Obstacle: Navigating cross-functional politics

Strategic alignment work often runs into the invisible walls of organizational silos. For example, people may resist coordination efforts out of fear of losing control, autonomy, or resources.

To navigate this, it's essential to focus on building trust first. This takes time, so be patient and remember that sometimes you must go slow to go fast. Or, as one of my mentors says, "slow is smooth, and smooth is fast."

When it comes to trust building across cross-functional teams, communication is key. Take time to listen. Approach your colleagues with humility and curiosity rather than trying to take control or impose your fantastic new ideas. And when you get to implementation, be sure to highlight shared wins. When people feel respected and heard, they're more likely to collaborate—and that's when real alignment can happen.

Of course, delivering rainmaker results is only half the battle; you also need to make sure your contributions are visible and recognized without alienating colleagues along the way.

Creating Visibility While Managing Relationships

As you've seen, each type of rainmaker move comes with its tactical challenges. But beyond these individual obstacles, there's a deeper layer of relationship dynamics you'll need to navigate to sustain success. These include managing upward, handling peer reactions, building cross-functional support, and ensuring your efforts are visible without alienating others.

Managing Upward Relationships

As you start making rainmaker moves, be aware that your boss may feel threatened, blindsided, or concerned. They may think you're moving too fast, too independently, or making them look out of the loop. This can happen no matter how secure and confident your boss appears. If you don't manage your boss well, your rainmaker ideas may not get implemented, and it won't be good for your career.

That's why you want to bring your boss along early and keep them updated. You're not asking permission but rather giving them "early looks" at your ideas so they feel involved and have a chance to provide input. I know as a boss, I hated having things sprung on me at the last moment when ideas were already fully baked. It's a lot harder to get someone's buy-in after the fact.

As you talk with your boss, position your ideas less as personal projects and more as ways to help them succeed. This is where framing your initiatives to align with a common goal (for both your boss and the organization) will make it easier to get their support, or at least keep them from blocking progress.

Navigating Peer Dynamics

Your rainmaker moves are likely to attract management attention. As you gain visibility, some of your peers may feel threatened or resentful. Others may feel jealous and compete with you or even feel the need to defend their territory.

While you can't control how others react, there are some things you can do to minimize the negative peer reactions. First and foremost, invest time to build informal alliances, ideally before the fact. If you don't have rainmaker ideas yet, that's fine—use this time to build relationships with your peers. Some of them will become trusted allies and partners, while others can be your eyes and ears on the ground. Just don't isolate yourself.

Again, when it comes time to present your ideas, it's all about the way you communicate them. Focus on why it's good for the organization and the impact it's making for the business and its stakeholders. Celebrate wins and acknowledge the other teams that have contributed. As the spokesperson (or even one of the spokespeople), you will get credit simply by association. You can afford to remain humble. And that's a good thing, because obvious "look at me" behavior usually backfires.

Cross-Functional Positioning

To make an impact on an organization, especially a large one, typically requires cooperation beyond your team. This means getting buy-in across departments and silos, which is often easier said than done.

This is where the skill of leading without authority comes to the forefront. To do this well means thinking like a diplomat. You can't order people around or rule by edict. It's about creating win-wins instead of power plays. The more listening you do—especially to understand the goals, priorities, constraints, and sticking points other units have—the better you'll be able to find where "what's in it for you" intersects for all teams. After all, self-interest remains the most powerful way to motivate people.

I suggest meeting with people from each group individually first to get the lay of the land. Then, you can call the relevant people together to develop ideas in what Judith Glaser (whom we met in the Introduction) calls co-creation.[14] When all the parties are involved early on, you're more likely to come up with an approach that everyone can support and that's hard for any one party to stop or sabotage.

Visibility Strategies

When you've had a great idea and driven the implementation, of course, you want to *make sure the right people know about your impact. You need that visibility to grow your career opportunities. But how do you do that without resorting to some awkward form of self-promotion?*

First, you can become an advocate for the initiative. Instead of promoting yourself, promote the rainmaker idea. If there are opportunities to speak to other groups that will be affected, take them. If you're better with the written word, see if there's a platform where you can publish a post or an article about it. For example, Wendy wrote an article for a trade journal and was interviewed for others.

When someone asks what's going on, take the opportunity to share the latest. A great way to do this is by creating a mini storyline that talks about the challenge, the solution, and the impact. For example, "You know how it's taken everyone months to get XYZ approved through the system? Well, the new Accelerator process we're rolling out next quarter should cut that time in half. It'll save the company $Y a year."

Second, make sure your allies and raving fans (who you'll meet in Chapter 10) are equipped with the narrative of what you've done so they can do some of the bragging for you. And third, share what's going on along the way so people naturally associate you with the rainmaker activity. Don't wait for the end to talk about what you're working on.

Just make sure what you say feels authentic to you and ties it to outcomes for the organization rather than for you personally.

Managing relationships while building visibility isn't about playing politics; it's about leading with emotional intelligence. By bringing others along, sharing credit, and staying anchored in what's best for the organization, you can show your potential and grow your impact without losing yourself in the process.

Putting the Creation of New Business into Practice

People who can expand the organization's set of opportunities are usually valued beyond all others. These are the rainmakers. To help you become one of them, work to hone your ability to create new business:

Rule 1: Identify the most important outcome(s) for your organization.

Think about what your organization must deliver to be successful. See if you can narrow this down to a few key outcomes (no more than three).

In professional services, it could be to make money for the firm by serving clients in the best possible way. For educators, it might be turning out a certain number of well-prepared graduates. For researchers, it could be creating new knowledge and publishing it. For an investment firm, perhaps it's delivering superior returns and keeping costs down.

In the market coverage group, my colleagues and I were judged by the client relationships we developed and, therefore, the revenue we generated from our client lists. At first, I thought that what mattered most was client relationships because the revenue opportunities sprang from those relationships. But then I noticed who was being celebrated in our morning meetings: the market coverage officers who brought in revenue-producing deals. There wasn't a lot of kudos for those hard-to-measure improvements in the relationships I was delivering. It wasn't until the department head's town hall meeting that I learned it wasn't just revenues that mattered. It was also the *source.* Revenues from winning new clients, which required a collaborative effort and opened up broader opportunities for the firm, were more valued than simply servicing "house accounts," the longstanding clients who would always do business with us. Understanding that not all revenues are created equal made me feel better about having a client list that was skewed toward new prospects because that allowed me to deliver those new clients to the firm.

Identifying the most important outcomes for your organization will give you clarity about where to focus your efforts.

Rule 2: Figure out how you and your group can contribute.

Using a machinery analogy, there is a certain number of levers an operator can pull to affect the output, and some are more powerful than others. The same goes for each of us in our organizations.

As a banker, my strongest lever for creating new business was to build client relationships. I could make the biggest difference through a combination of expanding our market share with existing clients and breaking into new client relationships.

For my colleagues in the controller function, it meant finding ways to streamline the process of providing the business units with real-time information so they could manage the business more accurately.

And in the case of a friend working in an African charity, it was to uncover an entirely new way to attract donations from a different pool of potential donors. For example, she teamed up with local artists and a London-based art gallery to host an art auction. This raised funds from art lovers, some of whom became ongoing patrons.

Once you've identified your most powerful lever, you're ready to move beyond just doing your job well—you're positioned to create new opportunities that didn't exist before. That's what separates the rainmakers from everyone else.

Rule 3: Create a safe space to test your ideas and practice.

Identify the network of people who can act as a confidential sounding board to help you "test drive" your ideas. You might bounce around ideas with trusted colleagues who are particularly open-minded, creative, and commercial. That's what I did. I had a handful of peers outside my immediate team with whom I had worked closely enough to know they could be trusted to give good advice and keep things confidential without risk of "stealing" my ideas ...

Timothy was my counterpart in the sales and trading division and was a great sounding board for understanding how stakeholders in sales and trading would perceive a proposal. Helen and Naomi were in the same unit as me, but on different teams. We bonded during a week-long leadership development program at Harvard Business School, where we represented the firm. They were the ones I turned to when I needed to gauge the level of interest for a women's event for clients and how best to present it for senior management support.

It's also helpful to get input from people beyond your immediate circle of confidants who can provide a broader perspective, especially if you need their buy-in to progress your ideas. As long as there are no confidentiality issues, there can also be an advantage to including external parties in your circle of trusted advisors. These could range from potential customers to subject-matter experts to wise mentors.

For example, after getting Helen and Naomi's input, I talked to a few senior bankers with clients we might want to invite to the client event. I also bounced the idea off a few of my female clients. Each conversation was a chance to practice and refine how I presented the idea. It was a great way to see which words and phrases landed best and incorporate what I learned into the next conversation (like the feedback loop from Chapter 4).

Having a group of people you can trust to test drive your ideas not only helps you gain valuable information, but it also helps you gauge whether you're on the right track. Better yet, these conversations further strengthen your relationships, which can provide advocates for your idea when the time comes to move ahead.

Rule 4: Learn from your network what will "move the needle" most.

As you develop ideas for creating new business, you may have more than one candidate to test out. For instance, there could be more than one thing that matters to your organization: growing revenues while keeping costs down or increasing customer satisfaction while also developing cutting-edge products. And for any one goal that matters to your organization, there may be multiple ways your team can contribute. For example, let's say you're in product development and the goal is revenue growth. There are at least two ways you could focus your efforts: take existing products and target them to a new customer base, or develop new products to sell to existing customers.

This is where you'll want to get input from your network on what direction to take.

Now, you may be thinking, *network—what network*?! If so, don't worry. Having a substantive reason to approach others is a great way to develop a network if you don't have one already and to strengthen the relationships you already have. After all, people are generally flattered when you ask for their advice. Plus, we'll cover more on networks in Chapter 10.

You want to get input from people who can give insight into which of your ideas will have the biggest impact on the organization. They need to be senior enough to have a broader perspective on whether an initiative will be seen as worthwhile and high-impact. Some of these people will be internal stakeholders, while others may be outside your group or organization. It all depends on who you think has the expertise and perspective you need.

This kind of input is essential because you don't want to waste your energy and resources trying to be a rainmaker only to find that you were working on the wrong thing... like focusing your efforts to expand the client base by developing relationships with startups when your organization is only set up to service big companies.

When it comes to approaching people to get a handle on what will move the needle most, it's best to do it in batches (versus all at once). If you have five or six people you want to get advice from, start with the two or three that are the most "user-friendly" or low-risk. Some may be easier for you to reach quickly, which is important if there's time pressure. Then regroup and see what you've learned and whether you want to test out a variation of your initial ideas. Progress to the more discerning audiences from there. This approach ensures you'll always have several people to learn from on the horizon.

Again, when meeting with people, remember to listen with an open mind rather than seek to defend your idea. After all, you should be meeting while your ideas are still malleable and not yet fully baked so you can incorporate what you've learned to strengthen your ideas and choose the one that will make the biggest difference. Making it an iterative process helps strengthen your idea into one that will really move the needle. All while getting buy-in, because people support ideas to which they feel they've contributed.

For a guide on how to approach people to test drive your ideas, check out the resources section (www.thevisiblebook.com/resources).

Make the Choice to Make It Rain

Every organization needs rainmakers—people who don't just do their jobs well, but who create new possibilities. The good news is you don't have to wait until you have a senior title or perfect conditions to start. You can step into that mindset right now, exactly where you are.

Start small if you need to. Ask better questions. Notice what's missing. Look for opportunities to create value where others see only tasks. Test ideas with trusted allies. Build momentum, one smart move at a time.

Rainmaking isn't reserved for a lucky few; it's a mindset and a practice. It's a way of seeing ... of leading. When you make that choice consistently, you change not only your career but the organizations and communities of which you're a part.

The world needs more rainmakers. Starting today, you can be one of them.

What's your next step to transition from caretaker to rainmaker?

PERSONAL ACTION PLAN

1. **Where do you see yourself on the caretaker-to-rain-maker spectrum, and what would it look like for you to move further toward rainmaker?** Reflect: Are you primarily executing what's assigned, or actively creating new value? What examples from your recent work demonstrate each mindset? What would "more rainmaker" look like in your current role?

2. **What is the most critical business outcome your organization must deliver to thrive, and how can your role contribute more powerfully to that outcome?** Consider: What keeps senior leaders awake at night? What would make the biggest difference to their success? What "levers" do you have access to?

3. **Which of the five rainmaker categories offers your biggest opportunity: Opportunity Creation and Expansion; Efficiency and Performance Enhancement; Problem Solving and Barrier Removal; Risk Mitigation and Future Proofing; or Strategic Alignment and Integration?** Think about persistent challenges you've noticed, untapped opportunities, or ways different parts of the organization could work better together.

4. **Who are 3-4 people you can approach to "test drive" your rainmaker ideas and get input on what would move the needle most?** Consider: Trusted peers for initial feedback, stakeholders who would be affected by changes, and senior people with a broader organizational perspective.

5. **How will you manage the relationship dynamics as you start making rainmaker moves?** Consider: How will you keep your boss informed and get their support? How can you build alliances with peers? How will you create visibility for your contributions without appearing self-promotional?

6. **Based on your reflections above, what's one specific rainmaker action you'll take this month to start creating new value?** Choose something concrete that moves you beyond just managing existing responsibilities toward expanding opportunities, solving systemic problems, or creating strategic alignment.

PART 3

WORKING ON YOUR
SELF

8

THE INNER GAME

Self-Awareness as
Your Career Accelerator

A client of mine, let's call her Susan, was hired to help with large change management projects at a Fortune 500 corporation. She had always been the upstart smart kid who came up with innovative approaches and successfully challenged the status quo because of her youthful passion, dedication, and the fact that her heart was in the right place.

However, the company she had recently joined was far more conservative and hierarchical. While Susan was now more senior with a leadership role where she could make a real difference for the company, she was frustrated that she hadn't been able to sell her ideas. She couldn't understand why her new colleagues weren't "getting it."

Worse yet, they asked questions she had considered but discarded three iterations ago. Didn't they know how hard she worked to provide them with the best solution—one tied with a perfectly coiffed bow? It made her angry to think about how ungrateful and stubborn they were being. But giving up was not part of her vocabulary, so she kept working hard to convince people of what she knew in her bones was the right way forward.

Finally, exhausted and exasperated, she asked a few colleagues for some feedback and discovered she was coming across as a "know-it-all," pitching ideas that would never work. From their perspective, the conversations she was having with them felt like one-way monologues. When they asked questions or expressed concerns, she didn't seem to listen. This was not at all what Susan had expected to hear. She had always considered herself open to new ideas, and her direct style of communicating, a plus. After all, it was seen as an advantage in previous organizations. Reflecting on this and after much discussion, Susan concluded three things:

First, she needed to manage her tendency to get defensive and argue when challenged. Instead, she would breathe, separate her "self" from the idea, mentally swivel around to their side of the table, and draw on one of the stock phrases we came up with, such as, "That's interesting. Tell me more about how that would work."

Second, she would leverage her special strength—the ability to envision a better way of doing things—but do it in a way where she could bring people along. That meant having conversations with others along the way to "co-invent" the solution rather than springing her full-blown conclusion on them at the end.

Finally, she realized that this group was not the most natural environment for her to shine, and that other parts of the organization would be a better fit for the long term. But working on these lessons would stand her in good stead in the meantime.

Once Susan implemented these changes and saw progress, her confidence grew, which in turn helped her be less defensive, more integrated into the group, and more effective in her role.

Susan's initial lack of self-awareness made her ineffective despite all the knowledge and good intentions she brought to the role. Grinding harder and doubling down on her efforts only made things worse. What she couldn't see was how she was contributing to the problem, let alone how to move forward. If left unchecked, it could have resulted in Susan being removed from her role, perceived as "damaged goods," which would dent her confidence and make it difficult to find another position within the company.

This can easily happen to any hardworking, well-meaning person, including you.

With Obstacles Come Self-Awareness

Even the smartest people can lack self-awareness. Whether busy, operating on autopilot, or too preoccupied to notice, it's not easy to see ourselves from the perspective of others. We all have our blind spots. But moments of challenge (like the one Susan experienced), or even disappointment, are opportunities for developing greater self-awareness—if only we care to see them as such.

You'll learn more from mistakes and setbacks than from when things are going smoothly. But it requires taking the time to reflect and assess. It also means not wasting time beating yourself up for getting things wrong or worrying that you'll never get back on track.

Self-awareness is about knowing yourself and what makes you tick. It's being able to manage yourself so that you can continue to learn, grow, and perform no matter what else is going on around you. Embedded in this is being grounded—knowing who you are and what you came here to do, and not letting things get to you or push you off track.

The Three Areas of Self-Awareness

When it comes to self-awareness, you must be aware of your tendencies, your strengths, and your best settings. As we saw from Susan's story, these can block your progress unless you consciously identify what they are.

As we go through each area, remember that self-awareness is a discovery process that stretches over your entire career. It's not something you can crack the code on once and for all; you'll want to revisit this capability regularly.

For example, I'm still discovering things about myself after multiple decades of work. From new ways my tendencies are getting in the way to new ways to apply my strengths to make a bigger impact, these discoveries are all making me a better colleague and leader. So, don't expect yourself to know the answers to all of them on your own.

And when you *do* feel like you know the answers, be open-minded. We are all changing as we go through our careers, just as the work we do and the expectations of us change. Every new situation reveals new aspects about our tendencies, our strengths, and the environments we feel comfortable in. It's like rotating a kaleidoscope; it's the same colorful pieces, but with each turn, the image looks different.

Area 1: Know your tendencies.

Tendencies are the natural way you approach a situation, especially one that's challenging or involves choices. Susan's natural tendency, for instance, was to double down on her position when she met with any resistance.

You can also think of tendencies as your natural preferences. For example, you may prefer the direct approach as opposed to providing a lot of explanation or setup before you express an opinion. Or you might tend to act decisively rather than step back and reflect before making a decision.

In a career context, it starts with getting to know what you're like at your best versus your worst. So, take a moment to envision what you're like at your best. Pull up from your memory bank a few key moments where you were proud of the way you naturally handled things, where you felt like you were in the flow or "in the zone." What do those situations illustrate about your tendencies?

Now, think about what you're like at your worst (what I call your stress personality). What brings it out? My stress personality is harsh, judgmental, and impatient. And it tends to come out when I'm hungry, tired, under deadline pressure, or uncertain about what to do next.

Hopefully, this little exercise illustrates why understanding your tendencies is the first essential step to managing them.

Put on Your Tendency Glasses

When it comes to tendencies, it's helpful to look at them through these lenses.

• Your Thoughts

What are your natural thought patterns—do you tend to see the negative or positive aspects? Do you have what psychologist Carol Dweck calls a fixed mindset, where you're limited in what change you can make? Or do you have a growth mindset, where you have agency and anything is possible?[15]

• Your Emotions

What is your default emotion? I like to think of the movie *Inside Out*, where there are five core emotions: joy, sadness, anger, fear, and disgust. When we watched the movie as a family, it was easy to recognize which emotion each of us tended to gravitate toward when we weren't paying attention. For me, it's mostly joy but also fear. This shows up as being the cheerleader who sees the "glass half full" in situations but also feels worried about how things will turn out or that I haven't done enough, which drains my energy and leaves me trying to get the thing perfect. How about you?

• Your Reactions

How do you react to positive results versus setbacks? Are you someone who celebrates wins or moves on to the next accomplishment? Do you feel like giving up at the first sign of obstacles, or do you double down and find a way to make it work? Are you the one who's calm, cool, and collected in a crisis or part of the group that's panicking?

• Your Actions

Do you tend to dive right in and start doing things or step back to think and plan? For example, the Kolbe-A™ Index assesses your natural tendencies to problem-solve in four areas: Fact Finder, Follow Thru, Quick Start, and Implementor.[16] A high Quick Start indicates someone who is comfortable taking risks, quick to jump into action, and thrives in situations requiring innovation and improvisation. Someone who's a high

Implementor excels in creating tangible outcomes from ideas and enjoys hands-on experiences in project-based environments. None of these natural tendencies is inherently good or bad. What matters is that you understand what comes naturally so you can make it work for and not against you.

Once you're aware of your tendencies, start noticing the impact you're having on others. Then, you can determine when and how to make adjustments. You might manage yourself in the moment. Or you might need to follow up with a colleague and apologize after realizing they were affected by your stress personality.

Area 2: Know your strengths.

When you're aware of your strengths, you can make informed choices that will lead to the greatest satisfaction and success in your career. You'll know what role to accept versus decline, which capabilities to invest in and grow as part of your professional development, which colleagues to partner with on a project, and what kind of talent to bring into your team.

Notice I did not talk about weaknesses. That's because leaning into your strengths generally gives you a greater result for the same amount of effort or investment. Of course, some weaknesses can become strengths if you focus on them; in which case, that's exactly what you should do. For example, learning French before your transfer to the Paris office could pay dividends, making it easier to connect with colleagues and clients and differentiating you from the other expats.

If you need to have a basic level of proficiency in some area of weakness, do what you need to do to get that weakness to become neutral, like learning the basics of reading a financial statement when you're put in a role with P&L (profit and loss) responsibility.

Otherwise, you're better off leveraging your strengths, which may include delegating a weakness. Let's say you're a great strategic thinker but not so good at paying attention to details. You might ask a team member or even hire someone to check for typos and fact-check your presentation. If you're too detail-oriented, on the other hand, you could consciously balance your need for detail with the larger picture by learning to delegate tasks where necessary, improving team efficiency.

Area 3: Know your best settings.

When I was reorganized out of a job, I was invited to look internally for another role and landed two offers: one in the prestigious and high-paying derivatives products group and another in the market coverage group. Everyone told me to take the derivatives role. It was aspirational, growing, and I would be in one of the hottest areas of the firm. I was flattered to be seen as worthy of joining that elite team. But it's one thing to get a job and another to actually do the job.

The derivatives team included some of the brightest minds in the firm. A handful were literally rocket scientists. They excelled at creating new products and structuring solutions to deal with some of the biggest financial risks our clients faced. None of these were on my list of strengths.

On the other hand, the market coverage role was about calling on clients for their financing needs and working closely with the corporate finance bankers who had senior-level relationships at those companies. This required a mix of interpersonal skills and an entrepreneurial mindset. To be successful, you had to be able to work collaboratively with internal and external stakeholders, communicate with influence, build trusted relationships, and bring in business without being sales-y. While I was untested in the business-generating part, everything else aligned with my strengths.

I ended up taking the less "sexy" market coverage role, which allowed me to lean into my strengths and shine. While the prestige and pay scale were lower than if I had taken the other role, I'm pretty sure I would have been at the bottom of the list of performers in derivatives, and it would have been a struggle to be average.

Remember, part of self-awareness is understanding the environment in which you grow best. Think of it as desert versus tropical hot house ...

Just as different plants thrive in different types of soil, each of us will do better in certain kinds of settings than others. Often, you can get a sense for whether a company or team is a good fit for you when you walk through the halls or talk to a large enough number of people who work there. Always trust your instincts. But there are also some specific areas to consider when it comes to figuring out what kind of environment will suit you best.

• The People

What kind of people do you prefer to work with, and what kind of pace do they operate at? I know I'm best working with people who are pragmatic, professional, and like to get things done. I like a fast-paced environment where things are constantly changing, and no two days are the same. You might prefer to be around people who are creative, faith-based, or fun, where there's time to think and plan.

One important caveat: Just because you get along well with someone doesn't mean they'll be great to work with or for. My client Lisa discovered this when she became a direct report of Kevin, someone in her social circle. The business unit Lisa headed up was being moved to another division, and she lobbied for it to report to Kevin, as they had always gotten along well. A year later, things were going so badly that Kevin was actively considering firing Lisa. It turns out there was a clash of work styles.

Kevin had a short attention span and expected his direct reports to keep him informed through short "fly-by" updates as they walked past his office. Lisa's legal background led her to prefer providing thorough updates in writing, followed by a meeting to go through the update point by point. She couldn't understand why Kevin kept canceling the hour-long meetings she asked for or cutting them short before she could get all her points across. Kevin hated receiving her three-page, single-spaced emails and the lengthy agenda that accompanied every meeting request. When they did meet, it was dry and sucked the fun out of the day.

So, keep in mind, when it comes to considering what people you prefer to work with, their work style is a big component.

• The Culture

Think of culture as the personality of the place you work. It's the set of behaviors, attitudes, and practices of the team, unit, or organization that collectively define what's okay (and not okay) within the group's interactions.

This set of norms, mostly unspoken and not written anywhere, can vary depending on which part of the organization you're in. This is because the people in the organization (especially the leaders) have a great deal of influence over the culture.

Culture can be hard to define. It's like the air we breathe. When we're in it, it's just how things are. But if we don't fit within the culture, we're like fish out of water. It makes it hard to move forward and excel.

Take Caroline, for example. When Caroline joined our group, she knew it would be challenging because she was leaving a regional firm to join a global bank. She knew there would be more pressure and higher revenue expectations, but she was up for the challenge. What she didn't anticipate, however, was that the traits that had been assets in her previous job were more of a liability in a more relaxed culture. Her dedication to the job wasn't coupled with a sense of humor and fun. When our group head told jokes in our morning meeting, Caroline didn't laugh along with the rest of us. She impatiently waited for the substance of the conversation. At a team-building dinner, she left abruptly when the guys broke out the after-dinner cigars. In the end, she left for another firm and thrived in a culture that suited her better.

If culture is the personality of an organization or unit, you do not want to clash. What kind of culture best suits you? Is it one that's aggressive, competitive, nice, or something else entirely?

• The Daily Tasks

If you're the equivalent of an orchid, make sure you take roles that provide a greenhouse environment; if you're more of a cactus, then even the toughest desert will do. In other words, no environment is inherently better than another. It's figuring out how to best align the nature of the work setting with how you do your best work.

I remember one junior analyst we hired quit after three months to take a job at an insurance company. We couldn't believe he had chosen what seemed like a boring job over the fast-paced, constantly changing position he held in market coverage. While we all thrived on the fact that our tasks and priorities for the day could change completely by 10:30 a.m., it turned out that he wanted to be able to get through his entire to-do list every day and go home feeling satisfied.

In what environment do you do your best work? Consider whether the requirements and associated tasks match, and whether there's enough variety or too much for your liking.

Removing the Obstacles

Self-awareness helps remove many of the self-induced obstacles that stand between you and greater success. Without self-awareness, you're at risk of falling way short of your potential by accident and not by choice.

That's because one of the greatest obstacles to achieving your goals is the fact that there can be a world of difference between your intention and how others perceive it. If you're unaware of how you're coming across to others, you could be leaving the wrong impression. Take the colleague who won't stop talking in a meeting, for example. He assumes he's the most interesting person in the room. In reality, everyone else is rolling their eyes at yet another boring monologue. You can bet that long-winded pontificator isn't at the top of the list of people to fast-track or include in a client meeting.

By being more self-aware, you're able to notice those self-induced obstacles—how you're being perceived by others—and adjust accordingly ... to ensure you won't fall short "by accident."

Moving from Self-Awareness to Self-Management

When things are going smoothly, it's easy and almost automatic to go from being self-aware to managing the way you show up smoothly, seamlessly, even automatically. Once you're aware of your tendencies and best environments, you'll be able to manage yourself to show up at your best most of the time, maybe even 80% of the time.

But there will always be extremes...

On one end of the extremes, there are high-pressure, high-stress situations, or times when you're so exhausted that you don't have the mental bandwidth to self-manage. For example, being in a high-stakes meeting where you're unexpectedly peppered with questions you're not prepared for, or being in a crisis where people are turning to you for answers and you don't have time to think.

On the other end of the extremes, there are times when you're so relaxed that you forget to self-manage and can get caught off guard. Take Olivia, for instance. She considered being at the office with her internal team as being "at home with family." She didn't realize that the way she responded to her colleagues was equally as important as the highly professional way she conducted herself with external clients. Her habit of sighing and looking weary when assigned work projects made colleagues reluctant to approach her. It earned her a reputation for being difficult to work with, despite the excellent quality of her work.

To give yourself the best chance of self-managing even in extremes, here are five strategies to experiment with.

Strategy 1: Trigger management

Anticipate the situations and people that are likely to trigger you in a way that makes it hard to self-manage in the moment. If possible, avoid putting yourself in those positions. When you do find yourself in those positions, have a plan in place for what to do when you notice you're being triggered.

Strategy 2: Recovery practices

Since you can't wrap yourself in cotton wool or control every situation, it's wise to put together a set of practices that can help you recover from those situations as quickly as possible. We're all going to fall or fail at times in our careers. It's inevitable. A big part of success is how fast you can get back up.

My favorite recovery practices include doing PQ Reps, which we talked about in Chapter 3, journaling, getting out in nature, and talking it out with someone I trust. What practices help you recover your composure?

Strategy 3: Energy management

Managing your energy is key to protecting your ability to self-manage in the moment. This is a preventive measure. It helps keep you out of high-stress extremes—but if you find yourself in their grip, it also provides a way to handle those situations so you can continue to be at your best.

For example, you might identify the times of day when you are best at particular tasks and plan your day around that. This preserves your energy, so you don't get exhausted and unable to perform at your best.

If you're looking for more ways to manage your energy, Simon Alexander Ong's book *Energize* is a great place to start.[17] And Jim Loehr and Tony Schwartz make a compelling case for managing your energy in their classic HBR article, "Manage Your Energy, Not Your Time."[18]

Strategy 4: Emotional regulation

If you're constantly experiencing emotional highs and lows, you know that it can be exhausting. This happened to me earlier in my career when I was transferred to London to start a new business. Without a full team to support me, I kept redoubling my efforts and worked way too many hours. I stressed myself out to the point that I came within inches of burning myself out.

Part of my recovery was working with a therapist, who asked me to graph my mood on a scale of one to ten for a couple of weeks. I was rather proud that my graph looked like a series of zigzags that covered the entire range. It turned out that pinging between big highs and big lows emotionally was not such a good thing, and it was happening because I had worked myself to exhaustion and wasn't sleeping properly. Managing those swings was the solution, which, for me, was through mindfulness practices and prioritizing self-care. What practices work well for you?

Strategy 5: Forming (good) habits

Adopting helpful habits can keep you from getting knocked off course by the extremes we all experience (this also helps with emotional regulation). James Clear has written about some highly effective ways to start and embed new habits in *Atomic Habits*.[19] My favorite is "habit stacking," or linking your desired new habit to an existing one. For instance, I added a new stretching habit to my morning routine (three years later, I still stretch immediately after brushing my teeth).

What are the habits working for you, and how can you leverage them? It might be your good bedtime routine or taking breaks during the workday.

What are the habits working against you, and how can you replace them with something better? For example, replace the habit of thinking only of the downside of the situation with the habit of zooming out and taking a balanced view of both the upside and the downside.

To make this shift from awareness to consistent self-management more systematic, consider creating your own Personal Operating Manual.

Your Personal Operating Manual

You have specific conditions under which you perform at your best, warning signs when things aren't going well, and recovery methods that work uniquely for you. Wouldn't it be handy to have an owner's manual to refer to, much like the one we have for our cars? It could help you ensure you're taking the right steps to operate at your best and walk you through troubleshooting when you're not. It could help friends and family, co-workers, and peers, too.

Turns out, the Personal Operating Manual does something similar—it's is a powerful tool for bridging self-awareness and self-management.

What Is a Personal Operating Manual?

A Personal Operating Manual is a document you create that captures your tendencies, preferences, strengths, and self-management strategies—all the things we've been talking about. It serves as both a tool for your self-reflection and potentially as a guide for others who work closely with you. By documenting these aspects of yourself, you make the implicit explicit and the invisible visible, which is a powerful step toward better self-management.

If you'd like to create one for yourself, you can download an editable Personal Operating Manual template at www.thevisiblebook.com/resources.

Putting It into Practice

Being self-aware and able to self-manage is a foundational capability that enhances your performance in all other areas. Here are four steps to take to improve:

Step 1: Gather data.

Our blind spots (both positive and negative) are what hold us back from achieving greater success and fulfilling our potential. We must constantly improve our ability to be aware of ourselves. How do we do that?

The Johari Window can help.[20] It's a tool for improving self-awareness, identifying blind spots, and enhancing mutual understanding between individuals and groups. The goal is to broaden the top left "pane" of the Johari Window, where you and others have a shared understanding about who you are and the value you bring. While you may need to be more open about yourself in terms of sharing your thinking and reasoning with others, the biggest opportunity typically comes from learning how others are perceiving you. That's where getting feedback from those you know and trust can be most productive.

JOHARI WINDOW

	I KNOW ABOUT MYSELF	I DON'T KNOW ABOUT MYSELF
THEY KNOW ABOUT ME	My open self	My blind spot
THEY DON'T KNOW ABOUT ME	My hidden self/ Their blind spot	Unknown unknowns

To get at others' perceptions, you'll need to ask some questions. They may include: "What do you see as my best strengths in a work context?" "Relative to others at my level, what do you see as my standout strengths?" "In my role as _____, what should I start, stop, and keep doing?" "In the context of running the team meeting, what could I do to make the session more effective?"

If you don't feel confident asking these questions, or you're afraid people won't feel comfortable giving honest answers, an executive coach can help by interviewing people confidentially and sharing the key themes with you.

Before you pose questions to others, it's helpful to take a cut at filling out the various panes in the Johari Window yourself:

- Top left pane: What feedback have you received from your stakeholders? What have you explicitly shared with them?

- Bottom left pane: What strengths, skills, and experience do you have that your stakeholders may not be aware of? What career aspirations have you not yet communicated to your managers, and which would be useful to share? What are the things you *don't* want to share with stakeholders?

- Top right pane: What perceptions of you might your stakeholders have, how accurate are they, and how well do they serve you?

- Bottom right pane: Well, those are currently unknown.

Here's a look at how I might approach this exercise. From prior year-end reviews, I knew I was seen as organized, hard-working, detail-oriented, humble, and good with people. These were important qualities, but the hallmarks of a "junior bear" are not the kind of characteristics that would help me advance very far beyond my current position.

What I wish I'd had the courage to let people know was that I had ambition—in fact, I wanted to be in the C-suite one day. I could be a good leader. I was also great at public speaking, but never had the guts to let my senior stakeholders know about any of this. Maybe it was imposter syndrome that kept me from speaking up. If so, I never wanted them to know about that lack of self-belief. That would be kept in the "hidden self" pane for the foreseeable future.

What I wish I knew was how my senior stakeholders saw me and my career prospects. And I'm sure there were plenty more things they knew but weren't telling me—some positive, others less so.

JOHARI WINDOW–EXAMPLE

	I KNOW ABOUT MYSELF	I DON'T KNOW ABOUT MYSELF
THEY KNOW ABOUT ME	• Organized • Hard working • Attention to detail • Good people skills • Team player	• How am I seen? • What's my next career step?
THEY DON'T KNOW ABOUT ME	• Ambitious • Good speaker • Good leader • Have good ideas • Imposter syndrome	?

As you fill out your own Johari Window, add the information you gather from your conversations or the themes your coach provides as you go. Also, don't ask just anybody. Inaccurate feedback can be even more damaging than no feedback at all because feedback is partly about the giver and their lens on the world.

For example, I once had a boss who told me I needed to have a shouting match to demonstrate to the guys on the trading floor that I was someone they should take seriously. But all I could think of was the time she went toe-to-toe with one of her colleagues in a shouting match. With her high-pitched voice, she sounded shrill, and the whole thing came across as ridiculous, mainly because it was so out of character. Despite her well-meaning advice, I decided to find my own way to get taken seriously.

Since even those you know, like, and trust can lead you astray, it's best to have a variety of people you can go to for advice. The choice of whom to ask depends on the situation. The more opinions, the more you can pressure test the advice you're hearing. But they all need to have your best interests at heart. They all need to be knowledgeable about the topic or situation and be able to communicate their thoughts constructively.

This is where it's helpful to have someone external to the situation but with contextual understanding so you can still gain valuable insights and advice. It could be a trusted peer, either inside or outside of your organization (which we'll talk about in Chapter 10, "Investing in Your Community of Support"). It could also be a third-party executive coach—someone … someone without a stake in the outcome whom you trust to give you their honest perspective.

Step 2: Reflect and notice.

Once you've gathered the data, it's time to step back, reflect, and see what you notice about the reaction of others to the things you say or do. How are they experiencing you, and how can you make use of what you're learning?

In my case, it was taking copious notes in meetings. I was mortified when my skip-level boss called me into his office, closed the door, and said, "Stop taking notes!" Apparently, it made me look like an assistant when he was trying to help me get promoted to managing director. I argued that it was to remember what was being said, and research showed that note-taking helps with information retention. He just looked at me and slowly repeated, "Stop. Taking. Notes." By the time I got over being defensive and shifted to jotting a few bullets on an index card, it was too late for that year's promotion. But I will always be grateful that he cared enough to give me that feedback.

As you go through this step, see if you can look at the data dispassionately. It's all too easy to feel defensive and dismissive, or to take it to heart and start beating yourself up about your missteps. Neither will serve you well in your career. So, resist the temptation to either discard it all as irrelevant or accept it all as completely true. Remember, feedback is partly about you and partly about the giver.

To make the most of the feedback you receive, choose one or two points to work on—being defensive when others challenge you, for example, or not speaking up in meetings. Then, as you go through the day, pay attention to when you exhibit those behaviors. Once you start noticing certain behaviors and when they kick in, you can choose to change them.

Step 3: Devise experiments.

Then it's time to act. The idea is to test people's reactions to your new way of doing, saying, or approaching things. You might also be testing out whether the feedback is accurate or which of the behaviors you're thinking of adopting feels most authentic.

Devising small experiments is the way to go for this one, which allows you to ease into a new behavior. I find it's best to conduct two to three at a time to speed things along. If you do experiments sequentially, one at a time, it will take longer to get the desired result. And choose experiments that don't "bet the farm." For example, introduce yourself to someone within 60 seconds of entering the room if you're shy, or notice when you find it hard to speak up and the reason behind it. Then test your theory in a low-stakes situation before deciding on the best way forward.

This is about testing out what behaviors work best for you, not putting your entire career at risk.

Step 4: Extract the lessons.

Every experiment yields valuable information, whatever the outcome. By experimenting, you'll start to lose defensiveness and open up to how others may see you, even if it's negatively. Then you'll be able to play with that data in a way that doesn't feel upsetting—but does help you advance toward your aspirations. So, keep track of what works well and learn from the failed experiments. In both cases, extract the lessons and move forward. The important thing is that you're taking action, learning, and improving.

The Foundation for Everything Else

Self-awareness and self-management form the bedrock upon which all other career capabilities rest. When you genuinely understand your tendencies, leverage your strengths, and create the conditions for your best performance, you unlock your full potential as a leader. This isn't just about personal development—it's about professional advantage. The mid-career professionals who invest in understanding themselves become the ones who can adapt to any situation, recover quickly from setbacks, and consistently show up as their best selves when it matters most.

In a world where technical skills can be learned and industry knowledge can be acquired, your ability to manage yourself with awareness and intention becomes your most sustainable competitive advantage. Every other capability in this book—from stakeholder management to team leadership to strategic thinking—depends on this foundation being solid. And when you're self-aware, grounded, and able to self-manage, you become comfortable in your own skin, which is the ultimate form of confidence.

PERSONAL ACTION PLAN

1. **What feedback do you need to gather about your strengths and blind spots?** Consider: What do you think you know about yourself versus what others might see? Who are two to three trusted people you can ask: "What should I start, stop, and keep doing?" or "What do you see as my standout strengths and potential derailers?"

2. **What are your core strengths and the "best soil" conditions where you thrive?** Reflect on: When have I been in flow or "in the zone?" What types of people, culture, and daily tasks bring out your best? How can you leverage these insights in your current role?

3. **What is your "stress personality," and what typically triggers it?** Think about: How do you think, feel, and behave at your worst? What situations or pressures activate these patterns? How does this impact your effectiveness and relationships?

4. **Based on your self-assessment and feedback from others, what are one to two key areas you want to work on?** Choose specific behaviors or tendencies that, if improved, would most enhance your effectiveness and career prospects. What small experiments can you try to practice new approaches?

5. **What self-management strategies will help you operate at your best more consistently?** Consider: How can you better manage your triggers and energy? What recovery practices work for you? What habits would support your optimal performance?

6. **What's one specific action you'll take this week to deepen your self-awareness or improve your self-management?** This could be gathering feedback from a trusted colleague, experimenting with a new behavior, or implementing a self-management strategy.

9

SHOWING UP AND STANDING OUT

Building a Presence and Profile That Feels Right

I was grinding my way through a long to-do list when my office mate turned and asked, "Did you see the memo?" Of course, I didn't. Yet another memo I missed because I was buried in my work. No doubt I looked confused, so he clarified, "The one about the karaoke charity auction at this year's Christmas party." He went on to explain that people would bid to hear each of us officers sing a song in front of the whole department. The money would go to charity. "Which song are you going to sing?"

I cracked open the memo and scanned the song list. I felt thrilled and terrified at the same time. Thrilled because I secretly loved singing karaoke, and one of my favorites, Gloria Gaynor's "I Will Survive" (which pretty much summed up my motto in life), was on the list. Terrified because I could not imagine revealing my inner diva in a work environment. I had worked too hard to cultivate my executive presence to be taken seriously. I didn't want my image to crumble at some silly Christmas party. Why would I risk embarrassing myself in front of senior management and the entire office? Like the separation of church and state, I kept a hard dividing line between my professional and personal lives, albeit with work taking up most of the real estate.

I practiced "I Will Survive" in the shower a couple of times, just in case, but decided I wouldn't sing.

On the night of the party, I arrived late (as usual) after finishing up a client proposal. The karaoke auction was already underway. Hovering in the back, I hoped to avoid notice and sidestep the entire event. Then my office mate Scott saw me and shouted, "I bid $1,000 to hear May Busch sing 'I'm Just a Gigolo' by David Lee Roth!" I was horrified for two reasons. First, a couple of our top management had stopped by to witness the festivities. Second, I didn't know the whole song. If I couldn't do something perfectly, I didn't want to do it at all. But, somehow, everyone seemed to think it would be hilarious to hear strait-laced May sing about being a gigolo, so I gritted my teeth.

When the bidding stopped at $2,000, Scott thrust the mic in my hand and pressed start. It was all going to charity; I couldn't say no. I muddled my way through the first verse, imitating David Lee Roth as he skipped and danced through the music video until the chorus, which everyone knew. My inner diva kicked in, and I pointed the mic at the audience. At the top of their lungs, everyone belted out, "I ain't got nobody, nobody cares for me, I'm so sad and lonely, (sad and lonely, sad and lonely) ..."

By the end, all 150 of us were singing, laughing, and having a great time. When the applause finally died down, my big boss came up to me and said, "You were great. People got to see a different side of you—fun, relaxed, relatable. You should have done that years ago!"

Instead of ruining my executive presence, this event had somehow added a "cool" factor to my brand. How lucky was I to have the entire department and senior stakeholders see me transform from a one-dimensional buttoned-up "goody-goody" to a multi-faceted, fun-loving person who's comfortable in my own skin?

I took away a multi-component lesson. Grinding away at work had taken me out of the loop. I was the last to hear the gossip. People didn't feel comfortable talking to me about anything that wasn't work-related. My perfectionist standards came across as prim, proper, and unapproachable. No one dared joke around with me, unsure how I might respond. Maybe they were afraid I'd turn them in for saying politically incorrect things. And I never got invited to go grab a coffee or "hang out." I was an outsider, never one of the gang.

... until I became visible ...

In the course of a single song, people started acting differently around me. They were more relaxed and friendly; they even cracked a few jokes—all because I had given them permission by showing my human side.

The Know, Like, and Trust Factor

No matter how competent you are in the technical aspects of your role, or how willing you are to work harder than everyone else, you'll have a hard time making your mark unless others notice, respect, and recommend you. For that to happen, they need to *know* who you are and the value you bring, *including your personal* and professional conduct, and *trust* that you're going to follow through on your commitments and keep confidences. Singing a song, engaging with the audience, and putting myself out there to raise money had satisfied all three of these requirements in one go.

It's the "know, like, and trust" factor that determines whether someone will advocate for you behind closed doors and recommend you for opportunities. It affects whether they'll keep you at arm's length or embrace you into their circles of influence. The thing is, not everyone will know, like, and trust you, and you don't need them to. When it comes to your career, it's the key stakeholders that you identified in Chapter 2 that matter most.

Enter Your Presence and Profile

This is where presence and profile come into the picture. They are "two halves of a whole" related to how you're coming across and being received by others:

Presence is how you show up when you're with other people. It's the way you carry yourself—how you present yourself in person to get people to take you seriously and earn their confidence and respect. It's also the vibe people get from you, the energy you bring when you're in the room, whether in person or virtual, and how well they can relate to you. This is often referred to as executive presence, and it helps to have it whether you're already an executive or not.

Profile is about how visible you are to other people when you're *not* with them. Making sure your reputation is known more broadly beyond your immediate circle. At some point in your career, it's not who you know; it's who knows you. Especially when it comes to your key stakeholders from Chapter 2, ideally, those stakeholders extol your virtues when you're not there and think of you when an exciting new opportunity comes up.

Not everyone has both presence and profile to the same degree. You can have a lot of one and little of the other. For example, an influential and award-winning academic can have a high profile but lack presence in a meeting (avoiding eye contact, stumbling over words, and being uncomfortable with small talk).

On the other hand, a highly competent lawyer can have great personal presence—run a tough meeting with confidence, command a room, and look the part—yet lack profile if no one knows who she is outside of her own department and client project team.

If you think that building your presence and profile are selfish pursuits, you can defer until later; stop right now. It's not simply about advancing your career. It's about doing what's good for the business and for your team. As product manager for one of our lesser-known financial products, it was my job to raise the profile of this offering both internally and externally. If our relationship bankers didn't know about me and my product, they weren't likely to talk to their corporate clients about it. Many other product managers were also clamoring for their attention. Those with the most trusted reputations got the airtime. If we weren't seen as a trusted provider in the marketplace, their clients wouldn't be as willing to do business with us.

When you show up in a way that commands respect, word will spread. When it does, you can help more people and deliver bigger outcomes, which creates a positive ripple effect on everyone around you.

People will want to work on your team. You'll be able to choose the best partners for your projects because people will be coming to you with proposals. You'll be in a position to do more business because word-of-mouth will be working in your favor, and that benefits your team and organization.

It's a winning combination.

What Presence and Profile Look Like

I could count on Ben to attend our group's morning meetings. However, he didn't "show up" in a way that gave him any oomph or presence. He would wander in sheepishly, holding a stack of papers, then sit in the far corner with his chair pushed away from the table. He had a quiet speaking voice and mumbled, so it was hard to hear him from the other end of the room, and he didn't look me in the eye. Instead, he often played with a paper clip as he talked. He also tended to preface his answers with tentative words like, "Um ... I'm not sure, but ..."

In contrast, Joan had a way of walking into the room with an air of confidence. The fact that she was tall and had great posture helped. She always sat at the table, alert and ready to participate. She had a neat Moleskine notebook, her phone, and a pen with her. When I called on her, I could count on her to present her update in a clear, concise way and make it sound interesting and engaging. Beyond that, she seemed comfortable in her skin and was even able to joke appropriately and get the group to laugh.

In other areas of the company that we dealt with, everyone knew Joan. This is where profile kicks in. When I went to client events in Joan's region, everyone knew her by reputation and respected her. Ben, on the other hand, seemed to be like those Olympic divers who make perfect dives—a clean entry into the water without making a ripple. While that's great for a career in competitive diving, it's not so good in careers outside of that sport.

Upgrading Your Presence

We all have ways in which we could easily undermine our presence without realizing it. For me, it was the habit of twirling my hair when I was stressed, which was most of the time. One of my colleagues adjusted his eyeglasses so often that it distracted people from hearing the substance of what he was saying. Others would jiggle their leg, rub their face, say "you know" every other sentence, or avoid eye contact. I even had a client who picked his nose throughout the meeting.

We each have a daily opportunity to enhance our presence in a meaningful way. There's no need for a big change or to undergo a personality transplant. I'm talking about looking for the small hinges that move big doors—leaving that stack of papers behind, for instance, or reeling in the need to take copious notes. You might upgrade your wardrobe to help you feel more senior and less like the junior bag carrier, which will allow you to be present in the meeting and make it easier to speak up (we'll touch on this further below).

By eliminating the nervous tics that undermine your presence and build up your Joan-like behaviors, you'll be surprised by how quickly you can shift perceptions and improve your presence so that others sit up and take notice ... in a good way.

Seeing Yourself as Others Do

But how do you know how you're coming across and which things to work on to move the needle the most? After all, it's hard to see yourself accurately. As much as it's up to you to act, the way others perceive you, by definition, lands in the "blind spot" pane of the Johari Window from Chapter 8. And in the words of my former mentor, "Perception is reality."

This is where feedback comes in.

If you want to rise within an organization, you need to be able to receive feedback—particularly the personal variety—without getting defensive or shutting down, so you can do something constructive with it. You must learn to listen to what you don't want to hear without getting upset. When you're upset, it's hard to hear what's really being said, and the other person is less likely to give you feedback again because of your reaction. The more reactive you are, the more you're seen as someone who can't handle being challenged, which will kill your chances of ever seeing the C-suite.

The key is to make yourself safe for others to give feedback to. It can be scary for someone to provide you with feedback because they don't want to hurt your feelings or have it taken the wrong way and ruin the relationship. Think of it this way: for them to get up the guts to give you the feedback makes it a gift ... so, be sure to receive their gift gracefully, not throw it back in their face.

This means saying "thank you" and not arguing. You can ask them to elaborate or give you an example if you're not clear about the feedback. But it's about adopting a stance of curiosity, not defensiveness. By making it a pleasant experience for the giver, they're more likely to share feedback again. That feedback is the key to your growth and future success. Without it, you're likely to stagnate in your career when it doesn't have to be that way.

That being said, don't buy into all feedback in the interest of being open-minded. Feedback is 50% about the giver; it's up to you to parse through it. Take the helpful parts and disregard the rest. Again, it's essential to get feedback from multiple sources, because no one person has the whole picture. The goal is to take various pieces of feedback and look for patterns.

Putting Presence into Practice

In my experience, four primary elements work together to deliver what we call "presence":

FOUR ELEMENTS OF PRESENCE

MINDSET	SPEECH
• Self-belief • How you "show up" • Feeling aligned at work	• How you speak • How often you speak • When you speak
BEHAVIOR	APPEARANCE
• How you sit/stand • How you enter a room • How you shake hands • How you take up space	• How you dress • Your grooming • Your default expression

Allow me to elaborate ...

• Mindset

Presence begins with mindset. As one of my coaching clients observed, it's working on your inner game to work on your outer game. This is because your mindset affects your behavior, which, in turn, affects your results. You can buy all the power suits you want, but if deep inside you still think of yourself as the junior bear or someone who doesn't deserve to be at the next level, that will show through and keep you from reaching your full potential.

So, get clear on how you want to show up. Work on your mental game and keep working on it. Don't get down on yourself if you're not feeling 100% all the time. No one does. No matter how successful someone is, they're still working on some aspect of their mental game. Don't ever think you're the only one who has worries or insecurities. Some of the most outwardly confident people experience imposter syndrome (I know because I've coached some of them), but they've found a way to deal with it.

Remember, you're not responsible for the first thought that comes to your mind, but you *are* responsible for what you do with it. So even if your inner monologue says that no one wants to hear what you've got to say, don't let that keep you from speaking up in that important meeting.

One of the things that's super important from a mindset perspective is to have alignment between the things you value and what your team and organization value. When the alignment isn't there, there's friction and conflict, which keeps you from doing your best work because it saps your energy and distracts your attention.

For example, you may value professionalism and producing quality work, but the rest of the organization values speed and "good enough" results. In response, you may find yourself spending extra time fixing what you see as your colleagues' shoddy work to meet your high standards. Not only does this mean you'll produce fewer (albeit better) results, but it's likely to cause frustration as your extra efforts won't be valued. They may even cause friction with colleagues who see you as stepping on their toes or taking too long.

You may also value getting things done, but your team values a strong work-life balance (which can lead to longer project completion times). You may value loyalty to customers and compassion for people, but your organization makes decisions—like discontinuing a product line or reducing employee benefits—based purely on near-term profits.

And you may value honesty when it comes to feedback, but the culture values being "nice" at all costs. It can be frustrating not to be able to give and get the honest feedback you and others need to be successful.

So, take a look at the things that you love about your work environment and the things that are draining you. See what you can do to resolve the exhausting aspects so you can give your attention to the areas where you can make a unique contribution.

• Behavior

First impressions. We all know how important they are. That's because our brains are wired to size someone up and form an opinion in a split second. Once formed, it takes work for our brains to let go of those opinions. With that, you might think of the behavior piece as watching a video with no sound.

Going to meet someone important for the first time? Take a moment to think about how you come across in a work setting. Consider yourself from an outsider's perspective, or you may create an impression that requires real effort for you to alter later.

What do I mean?

Once upon a time, I went to a senior-level client meeting with one of my team members. I was heading up the European team, and my head of France, let's call him Quentin, asked me to join a meeting with the finance team of a particularly important client. A lot of money was riding on this deal. As group head, my role was to bring gravitas and assure the client we would deliver as a firm.

We were ushered up to the conference room, Quentin leading the way. As we entered, the CFO peered over Quentin's shoulder and asked whether I was the new junior analyst. Quentin replied, embarrassed, "No, she's my big boss."

My French was good enough to understand this exchange, and I was mortified. Let's just say it was hard to do the gravitas thing after such a weak start. Something would have to change if I didn't want to find myself undercut again.

At five feet two inches, the first change I made was to enter the room first, if possible. This ensured I would not be hidden from view behind a tall team member or colleague. Second, I developed a way to enter a room with confidence, sailing in with a smile, and extending my hand to greet the most senior client with a personalized compliment I prepared the day before. Clients found it disarming that I knew their most recent accomplishments, and it gave me confidence to speak up in the room from the start.

Then, having made my entrance, I would choose a seat that reflected my seniority level, where the senior-most client and I could easily see each other. And I took up my space at the table, making sure there was ample room to lean forward, spread my elbows out, and make a wide gesture with my hands to make a point if I wanted to.

This new way to show up served my team and clients better and enhanced my reputation both internally and in the market.

When it comes to behavior, start to notice the things you do. This could be the way you sit or stand, your body language, the way you move through space, and how much space you take up. For ideas, start looking at others for behavioral cues that you could emulate and make your own.

Speaking of behavioral cues, I want to take a moment to talk about handshakes. While they've been replaced by fist bumps or a simple head nod for many, there's still merit to a good handshake.

The reason a handshake is so important is that it is the only form of appropriate touching in the business world. It adds to the richness of information you learn about each other. Someone might look confident, but if their palms are all sweaty, that's a tell. As in poker, it reveals they're probably not as confident as they may appear. On the other hand, that person with the bone-crushing handshake may be telling you that he has the need to dominate or overcompensate for some kind of insecurity. And a limp fish handshake? In a business setting, nothing says "pushover" louder.

• Speech

Think of this as listening to the soundtrack of a video with your eyes closed. This is about both how you speak and when you speak. For one of my coaching clients, this is at the heart of what's holding her back from achieving the executive presence she needs to advance in her career. Her cultural background leads her to be respectful of hierarchy, making it challenging to speak her mind and push back on the senior management team's views, even when she disagrees. She also struggles to get involved in the debate when other colleagues are more assertive about taking up their airtime. But if she's asked to speak, she does a brilliant job of it.

For one of my colleagues, the verbal aspect that undermined their executive presence was their tendency to preface points with apology language—"I'm not sure this is right, but ..."

Others tend to rush through what they're saying when they're nervous. They can't wait to get to the end, so they say it all in one breath. Hardly the mark of a confident professional on the rise.

To identify where you stand in terms of speech, start to notice what you sound like as you go through the next day.

• **Appearance**

If behavior is like watching a video with the sound off, and speech is like listening to the soundtrack, then appearance is a still photo. It's what you're wearing, your expression, clothes, and grooming. All of these are on display and say something about your presence without you ever having to say a word.

For example, what would a short skirt, five-inch stilettos, and a low-cut blouse lead a stranger to believe about your colleague? What about a tight bun, conservative dress, and patent leather pumps—how would that stranger view your colleague now? Depending on the context, either one could be the most appropriate. The main thing is to be aware and intentional about how you're showing up.

As much as it feels unfair to be judged on appearances, the human brain can't help but size someone up in a split second. Just as books are judged by their covers, you and I are judged by initial impressions, too. That's why it's best to get it right from the start. I know this to be true because my physical presence (or lack thereof) kept me from getting promoted to managing director the first time around.

The trading floor was deserted, but I was still grinding away at my desk when my skip-level boss came by. Leaning back in the swivel chair at the desk next to mine, he looked at my white cotton shirt and boxy navy suit, then down at my scuffed-up shoes, and back up at my outfit and said, "You need Jil Sander." Having been mistaken for a flight attendant at the airport the month before, I knew my wardrobe needed an upgrade. But work came first, and shopping never even made it to the top half of my to-do list.

Thinking this was a personal shopper, I said, "Thanks, give me her number and I'll call her tomorrow morning." He leaned forward in the chair, grabbed my pen, and wrote JIL SANDER on my notepad. He mistakenly thought I misheard the name, given his accent. When I said I understood and asked for her number again, he stood up and signaled me to follow him across the trading floor. He asked every woman who was still there, "Who is Jil Sander?" Every single one, even the temp answering our phones, knew that Jil Sander was the fashion designer known at the time for women's power suits.

Looking back, it's clear that my skip-level boss had floated my name for promotion but got the feedback that I lacked the presence and gravitas of a managing director. The clothes and grooming were vital if I was to look and act the part. Thankfully, this was easy to change. And I discovered that once I was wearing the next level wardrobe, I naturally started to behave in a more senior way.

Where to Start Developing Your Presence

Figure out which area is most important for you to work on *right now*. It could be the area where the biggest gap exists between where you are and where you want to be. On the other hand, it could be the area that would give you the most confidence if you were to address it. The most important thing is to choose one aspect and start.

Profile is Born of Presence

Once you've addressed your presence, it's time to build a higher profile and raise your visibility. What's the difference? Presence is how you come across when you're in the room; profile is the ripple effect you create beyond being together in person, whether face-to-face or virtual. Presence is how you're perceived when you're in the company of others. Profile is how widespread people's knowledge of you is. The two work hand-in-hand.

Why You Need to Develop Your Profile and Visibility

This is essential if you want to be considered for opportunities that allow you to make a bigger impact. But for much of my career, raising my profile felt challenging. Maybe you can relate? It felt like a bridge too far to go from my "nice Chinese girl" training (being humble, hardworking, and not making waves) to becoming what I thought of as a public relations machine who had no problem bragging, brown-nosing, and self-promoting at the drop of a hat. This held me back in my career until I finally realized the following ...

Developing a high profile isn't selfish. In fact, it's exactly the opposite. It's your *duty* and *responsibility* to raise your profile, especially as you get more senior. Your team is counting on you to be visible and respected so you can successfully advocate for them. Your unit needs you to have a high profile to attract the best business opportunities and get support from other units to make them a reality.

Your organization benefits from your being visible so you can more effectively advocate for the mission and be better able to deliver results. You benefit, as well—from enhanced career opportunities that are more fulfilling to better support your family and the causes you care about most.

To get the kind of profile you need to keep advancing (and fulfill your potential), you cannot be the best-kept secret. You need to put yourself out there. This quote from marketing professor, psychologist, and advertising consultant Steuart Henderson Britt sums it up: "Doing business without advertising is like winking at a girl in the dark. You know what you are doing, but nobody else does."

What Are You Known For?

When it comes to your profile, consider how you *want* to be perceived, which is the brand you want to convey, versus the way you're *actually* perceived, which is your reputation in the eyes of others. To the extent there's a gap between your brand and reputation, you'll want to close it. (Going back to the Johari

Window in Chapter 8, the way others perceive you is in that "blind spot" pane until you find a way to discover it and shift it to the "open self" pane.) Getting that alignment is the basis for developing a profile you'll be happy with.

I remember the year-end self-evaluation where I proudly listed my three greatest strengths as being a good leader, being good with clients, and being organized. However, the feedback from stakeholders in my 360 end-of-year review told a different story. My seniors, peers, and juniors saw me as hardworking, detail-oriented, and organized. At least we agreed on my organization, but the more important skills weren't on anyone else's list. The strengths I was known for could be true for my amazing administrative assistant, but I was aiming for the C-suite. I couldn't believe how off-base my self-perception was to reality. Talk about a giant blind spot. This was the wake-up call I needed to start working on my profile. What might be the gap for you?

Rather than waiting for a formal year-end review, one practical way to figure out your brand versus reputation gap is to come up with the three words or phrases that you'd like to convey as your brand. Then, ask three to five people who know you well (and whose judgment you trust) for the three words or phrases that come to mind when they think of you professionally. The difference between your answer and theirs is the gap. And being aware is the first step to changing those perceptions.

As for those with whom you need a high profile, a good place to start is with your Stakeholder Map from Chapter 2. These are the people who need to know who you are and what you bring to the table. In many ways, these internal audiences are easier to build your profile with because you know who they are, and you're likely to have regular opportunities to get in front of them in a visible way.

But you'll also benefit from building your profile externally, beyond the circle of people who have some knowledge of you already. External audiences could be outside of your organization. They could also be within your organization but outside of your unit. Becoming more visible with this broader group might sound daunting because you won't necessarily know who these individuals are. They could be prospective clients, other industry players, or potential employers. How do you even start?

To make it doable, simply find energizing ways to put yourself out there. If you enjoy being in front of an audience, then consider giving a talk at an industry conference. If you're passionate about your area of expertise, get some media training and start getting quoted in the press, leverage social media, or speak at conferences. If you care about a particular cause, maybe take on a leadership position in your company's employee resource group on the topic.

Start by looking at the places where you're already active and take it up a notch. You never know where it could lead. For one of my colleagues, her interest in sustainability showed up initially as putting together a strategy for sustainable investing and ultimately led to a broader role as the firm's first chief sustainability officer, making an impact through founding major sustainable finance initiatives across the industry.

If you're planning to attend an industry conference, consider offering to speak or participate on a panel. Not only will the people attending your session get to know you, your photo and bio will also be on the conference website and marketing materials, which gives you far more reach than blending in with every other attendee.

If you're writing white papers or thought pieces for clients, how about sharing a public-facing version of that on your LinkedIn page? Not only will this spread the word about your organization's capabilities, but you'll also boost your reputation as an expert and thought leader in the subject, which could lead to more opportunities for you and your team.

Developing Your Purposeful Profile

Developing your profile doesn't need to be filled with a "yuck-factor," and you don't need to sell your soul. It's important to frame (or reframe) it as the important professional skill it is. It's not gaining profile for the sake of it. We're not talking about developing the fame of a social media influencer. It isn't about becoming known to build your ego.

You're aiming at developing a profile that fits your purpose. This is why I think of it as developing your *purposeful profile.* It's building your visibility with integrity and gaining the recognition you deserve without compromising who you are. It's how I (and many like me) have been able to understand, appreciate, and implement this critical leadership skill and feel good about it.

Here are three strategies that work well:

Strategy 1: Put yourself out there.

Show up and speak up. This is directly linked to your presence when you're in the room with others. Think about what kinds of meetings or events you attend and the informal conversations you're a part of. Do you make it a priority to show up to gatherings, whether formal or informal, or are you mostly sitting at your desk grinding away at your to-do list?

This doesn't mean attending every event or meeting, but it does mean being intentional about making the time and effort to show up in the places and spaces you want to be part of, whether that's in person, virtual, or in written communications. Find ways to make it doable and authentic. For example, if you're on the way to a town hall meeting that you know your skip-level boss is also attending, ask if she wants to walk over together. When someone speaking on a panel offers to follow up with those who contact them, be one of the few to email them requesting a brief meeting.

Strategy 2: Own your narrative.

Create the storyline you want others to say about you. Humans are wired to tell and remember stories, and these narratives are powerful in shaping perceptions and decisions.[21] It's how information was passed from generation to generation before the written word was invented. Whether we know it or not, others will have formed stories about us and vice versa. We also have stories about ourselves. The key is to be aware of them and keep them current so we can ensure they're helping us move forward in our careers and lives rather than holding us back.

In my case, it was the "nice Chinese girl" narrative I mentioned earlier in this chapter: keep my head down, work hard, do an excellent job, don't make waves, and good things will happen. Based on my year-end evaluations, I'm pretty sure that's the story my managers and colleagues had of me, too. The way I behaved shaped their stories about me. While it helped me advance early on when I was in the trenches grinding out the work, it became a showstopper when I wanted to advance to higher-level roles.

This is where owning your narrative comes in. Instead of the default storyline others might have about you, it's up to you to identify what you want the narrative to be. And then "live into" that story by behaving that way consistently so that becomes their experience of you and the way they see you.

In my case, that meant replacing the "nice Chinese girl" story I had for myself with the narrative I was growing into: a confident, commercial, and leader-like professional able to win over even the most difficult clients. As I adopted that narrative, I felt myself becoming more confident, commercial, leader-like, and effective with challenging clients—just as dressing at the next level up helped me behave like a leader. It showed up in the language I used. There were no more caveats like, "I may be wrong about this, but..." or "this might be totally off base, but..." It showed up in the way I sat up in meetings and strode through the hallway. I became more intentional about spotting revenue-producing opportunities. I approached challenging client situations with curiosity rather than fear, which allowed me to stay calm and not get rattled. And that made it easier for me to win them over.

For you, the narrative might include being a systems thinker who finds solutions to complex problems, or the calm, strategic leader who keeps their cool when things are going wrong. Whatever it is, own that narrative, live into it, and people will start to see you in a way that serves your career and your ability to make a greater impact in the world.

Strategy 3: Dare to be different.

Have a point of view and leverage your uniqueness. It's human nature to want to belong, and that can lead us to conform to group norms. I've come to see that organizations are like large planets with a huge gravitational pull toward the center—to stay in line, to fit in. Much of the time, this is useful. Your team, your department, and the entire organization need to move together toward a common mission, like birds flying in formation as they head south for the winter. You don't want to be the lone bird fending for yourself.

But all things taken to extremes can become negatives. This is where it's important to know when you need to fight that gravitational pull to look, sound, act, and be exactly like everyone else. The question becomes: within your organization, what is your point of differentiation? What do you uniquely bring that no one else provides quite like you do?

Take one of my clients, for example. Everything about him was conservative, from his navy suit and white shirt to his wing-tip shoes. But one look at his distinctive eyeglasses—bold, artistic frames—and you knew he was someone with design sense and creative flair. All the more interesting because his day job was treasurer of a multinational corporation. Those glasses became his signature, a conversation starter that revealed depth beyond the numbers.

Or consider my former colleague who had a gift for bringing up ideas that were dramatically different from the norm. He could present unconventional thinking in a way that others could rally around, or at least not reject out of hand. His willingness to voice what others were thinking but afraid to say made him invaluable in strategy sessions.

The key is the 80/20 rule. If you're 100% different, people won't be able to relate to you. But showing that distinctive 20%—whether it's your unique background, your willingness to voice necessary truths, your authentic communication style, or your point of view on the business—is vital for standing out and being remembered for the right reasons.

Make Your Profile Matter

The goal of these three strategies isn't to turn you into a self-promotion machine or a corporate politician. It's about leveraging what makes you unique in the service of better outcomes. When you put yourself out there authentically, own a narrative that reflects your true strengths, and dare to show what makes you different, you're not just building your profile—you're often providing exactly what the team or organization needs, even if they didn't realize it.

Remember my karaoke moment? I wasn't trying to be different when I got up there—I was being authentically myself. That willingness to show a different side, to be human and vulnerable, completely shifted how people saw me. It permitted them to be more relaxed and real around me, too. In one song, I had put myself out there, owned a new narrative about who I was, and dared to be different from the buttoned-up executive they thought they knew.

Your profile-building doesn't have to be dramatic. Sometimes it's as simple as being the person who always follows through when others make empty promises, or being genuinely curious about people's ideas when others are just waiting for their turn to talk. Sometimes it's speaking up in a meeting when you have valuable insight, even if it challenges conventional thinking.

The point is, don't hide what makes you valuable to blend in. Instead, find ways to let your authentic strengths serve your purpose and add value to those around you. That's how you build a purposeful profile that advances your career while staying true to who you are—and that benefits everyone around you in the process.

Showing Up as Your Best Self

Developing your presence and profile is not a selfish endeavor that's just about you. It's an essential skill that benefits your team, your organization, your clients, and yes, even your family. Yet, the "how" of achieving the result rests squarely with you.

This isn't about becoming someone you're not—it's about showing up as the fullest, most effective version of who you already are... and who you're becoming. Every small improvement in how you show up, every thoughtful step to build your reputation, every moment you choose authenticity over playing it safe compounds over time. The karaoke moment that transformed how my colleagues saw me wasn't about perfect performance; it was about having the courage to show up and be real.

You don't need to wait until you feel completely confident or have achieved some imaginary level of perfection. Start
where you are, with what you have, and let your genuine value
shine through. The world needs more leaders who combine
competence with authenticity, and you're perfectly positioned
to be one of them.

As the saying goes, be yourself—everyone else is already
taken.

PERSONAL ACTION PLAN

1. **Assessing your current presence across the four areas (Mindset, Speech, Behavior, Appearance), where do you feel strongest and where do you see your biggest opportunity for improvement?** Consider: How do you show up in meetings? What nervous habits might undermine your presence? How aligned do you feel with your work environment?

2. **What three words or phrases do you want to be known for professionally, and how does this compare to how others likely see you now?** Test this by asking 2-3 trusted colleagues: "What three words come to mind when you think of me professionally?" Look for gaps between your desired brand and current reputation.

3. **Looking at your key stakeholders from Chapter 2, with whom do you most need to build the "know, like, and trust" factor?** Consider: Who needs to know your value? Who might not feel comfortable around you? Who questions whether you'll follow through on commitments?

4. **What's one specific way you can "put yourself out there" to build your purposeful profile?** Consider: Speaking up more in meetings, attending industry events, sharing expertise on LinkedIn, volunteering for visible projects, or taking on leadership roles in employee resource groups.

5. **Who can help you develop your presence and profile by providing honest feedback and accountability?** Think about: Colleagues who can give real-time feedback on your presence, mentors who can advise on profile-building opportunities, or trusted peers who can help you practice new behaviors.

6. **What's one specific action you'll take this week to build your presence and profile?** Choose something concrete that addresses your most significant opportunity from the questions above.

10

YOUR COMMUNITY OF SUPPORT

Creating a Network of Career Champions the Authentic Way

My client Ted was looking for the "next right role"—one that would get him back on a corporate track after the detour he took into arts management. The higher income would be important now that he and his wife were expecting their first child, and they wanted to move back to New York, where they had family.

Coming from a musical family, Ted hadn't been able to resist taking on the challenge of working on the turnaround of a performing arts center on the West Coast. He delivered on his part of the project quickly and immediately began chomping at the bit for his next challenge. Unfortunately, the management structure of the organization held limited opportunities in the near term. Unless his new boss moved on or something else changed, Ted was stuck in middle management for the foreseeable future. This is why he began considering his other options. With a young family to consider, Ted felt the need to get his career back on an upward trajectory during his prime earning years.

Before this, Ted had had a strong start to his career. After graduating from the Air Force Academy and earning an MBA from Kellogg, he joined an aerospace firm where he was promoted rapidly. Fortunately, Ted had kept in touch with colleagues and former mentors along the way—a coffee here, a call there. Helping a mentor's daughter with her application to the Academy a few years ago had also turned out to be a great investment in keeping his community fresh and eager to return a good deed. Plus, being connected on LinkedIn made it easy for Ted to keep track of those supporters who were less frequent contacts.

When it was time, Ted put together a game plan, reached out to his community, and was able to uncover multiple leads that put him well on his way to getting that "next right role." Ted understood the payoffs of building your community (a significant percentage of jobs are found through connections and networking). Instinctively, he'd made staying in touch with helpful people with little to no nexus to the arts a personal priority, just in case.

Such a support network serves as a safety net in times of need and as your accelerator when things are going strong. Regardless of the twists and turns your career makes, never forget the encouraging, helpful people you've met along the way. They can serve you (and vice versa) in surprising ways.

The Power of Allies

It can be a cold, hard world out there, particularly when we're climbing the ladder. We all need people we can trust to help us along the way: people we can turn to; people who "have our back"; people who rate us highly and recommend us. These people serve as potential allies.

My counterpart in the sales and trading division, Timothy (whom you met briefly in Chapter 7), was one such ally. When I needed to make the case to senior management for entering the lending business, which was highly unpopular, Timothy was able to get the powerful derivatives group to throw their weight behind it as well. Having this support added to the credibility of the case, and we ultimately won approval.

Then there was the time when our new CEO asked to meet with me to understand what value my group added and why it should remain in place. In essence, I had to justify the existence of my group. When I entered the conference room, he was already seated at the head of the table with his top five lieutenants flanking him on both sides. Less than a minute into my presentation, he interrupted with questions. The grilling had begun. Now, I'm fine with questions, but he was asking the *wrong* questions—ones that showed he had a misunderstanding of what my group did. I looked around the table for support, but nothing... the pre-meeting conversations I'd had with each of the lieutenants, where they had agreed to support my program, were for naught. So, I turned to the CEO and said, "That isn't exactly what we do, but I guess you want me to answer the question anyway ..." That's when one of the lieutenants, who was my former skip-level boss, spoke up to clarify my group's role. That broke the tension and bought me precious moments to gather my thoughts. I was able to get the meeting back on track and left with the CEO's approval.

Through incidents like this, it becomes clear who your true allies are—who have your back, even when things are challenging. Perhaps *especially* when things are challenging. As Warren Buffett famously said at the 1994 Berkshire Hathaway shareholders meeting, "Only when the tide goes out do you discover who's been swimming naked." In this case, it's only when the going gets tough that you know who your true allies are.

I will always be grateful to my former skip-level boss for stepping in. It highlighted for me the importance of staying in touch with people even when they're no longer a direct stakeholder and how vital it is to cultivate trusted relationships.

Unlike family, you can choose who's in your community as well as whose community to be a part of. You might call them your connections or your network. Most often, you'll see me use "community of support" simply because I feel "network" is overused and often seen as shallow and icky, like self-promotion.

From a professional standpoint, the people in your community of support aren't necessarily your friends. They're the set of personal contacts, affiliations, and relationships you have. They could be fellow alums from college or a previous employer, people you enjoy working with, a former boss who has always looked out for you, people you've met at conferences, or your buddy at the gym.

While you will know some of them better than others, your community of support is made up of people you can reach out to for information, advice, support, and access to opportunities—and vice versa. Some of them will be stakeholders from Chapter 2 who can directly influence your rise in your organization. Others will play a less direct role in your career advancement.

While there's overlap between your community of support and your stakeholders, the two are not identical. Your stakeholders are people you have to deal with. They may or may not like, trust, and respect you, and vice versa. For example, that jerk in finance whose input you need to get your job done is a stakeholder but not someone you'd choose as a member of your community of support or otherwise see as an ally.

For now, I'm going to assume you already have some of the building blocks for your powerful network. But let's be clear on the types of people you'll want in your circle and why, so you can ensure a far easier rise to the top.

Roles to Fill

Within your community of support, several roles are particularly valuable. You may find that some of the people in your community play more than one role, and you may have roles yet to be filled. In which case, you'll need to shop for someone to fill it.

Take inventory. You might jot down a few names to see where you are well represented and where you need to address gaps.

- **Sponsor**

A sponsor is someone who actively advocates for you and looks out for your career. When it comes to your sponsor, you want to consider what part of the organization they're in and how it relates to your area ... if their star is rising or falling ... how much longer that person will be in a position to sponsor you. For example, if your sponsor is nearing retirement or likely to be promoted to a different part of the organization, you may need to build relationships to find a new one soon. There's also the danger of hitching your wagon to the wrong person.

You may recall the story of my senior manager, who was a rising star and had taken me under his wing. When he got promoted to a different department, he brought me with him as his right-hand person. It was all going well when I went on maternity leave, or so I thought. Four weeks later, he called me in to help with an urgent restructuring of the group. Turns out my sponsor's star had fallen, and he was the one being restructured... right out of a job. Having worked closely with him for six years at the exclusion of anyone else, I found myself left out in the cold and in need of a job as well. Ultimately, I landed a role that better suited me, but never again would I allow myself to be so closely tied to any one person. Neither should you. This is why I'm taking the space to repeat this lesson.

• Mentors

We all need mentors—people who have greater expertise, experience, and wisdom than we do in a particular area and are willing to share their advice and guidance. You'll want a variety of mentors to cover the areas where you would most benefit from advice. For each topic area, it's ideal to have more than one mentor so you're sure to reach at least one when needed and have multiple perspectives.

Most of us benefit from having a few general career mentors and a larger number of mentors we can turn to for specific aspects of our personal and professional development. They can help navigate organizational politics, deal with parenting challenges, manage a problem team member, and so forth.

Mentors come in different styles and backgrounds, which is why it's best to have more than one person you can turn to for whatever situation you're looking to address. For example, when I needed some strategies for dealing with a challenging client situation, there were a handful of senior bankers I could call on for advice. Some were most helpful in the context of handling complex negotiations, while others were best at client relationship-building strategies.

Just as it's helpful to have a deep bench of talent on your team, you'll benefit from having a deep bench of mentors to call on.

• Peer Coaches

People at your level, with whom you share a relationship of trust—to give each other confidential feedback, share strategies, and exchange ideas and information without fear that it will be used against you—are your peer coaches.

They are especially useful for behaviors you are seeking to change. For example, a colleague who attends many meetings with you can give you a signal when you are talking over a client. It's also helpful for navigating the politics of the organization, like a peer who can help you make sense of conflicts that pop up during the week.

When it comes to good advice, it helps to have people who are knowledgeable about you and familiar with the situation you're facing, but who can also be impartial. This is where the push-pull comes in. You can trust your family and friends to have your best interests at heart, but they may not fully understand the work context. Like the time I called home in a panic because I had lost three hours of work when my computer crashed, and there was no way I would meet a big deadline.

Somehow, I knew my mother's suggestion to "just put on a big smile and it will be okay" wouldn't quite cut it.

The people you work with will have the knowledge, but it's hard for them not to be biased. The challenge is knowing which peers to trust to give good advice *and* keep things confidential. And it's probably safest to confide in people who don't interact with the people you work with.

It's ideal to have an external group of peers who are at your level and going through similar things but aren't in your daily work circle. For example, one of my coaching clients meets with a handful of former business school classmates who are also in finance but working in different organizations. In my case, remember those two women I bonded with during a week-long residential leadership program? We still call on each other decades later.

If you didn't leave school with an enviable list of long-term relationships or have the chance to develop beneficial alliances at some work-related program or retreat, don't worry. You can still find trusted peers in a third-party program like my Career Mastery Leadership Accelerator, which carefully curates a small group of professionals across geographies and sectors who help each other advance and become better leaders. We get to create our own luck at any point in our careers.

Even if you don't have access to a "ready-made" curated group and you only have access to internal peers, you can still form a trusted group of peer coaches on your own. The trick is to start slowly because trust is built over time.

A good first step is to identify people with whom you feel comfortable. Maybe you like their energy; perhaps you sense a kindred spirit. Then test out the quality of their advice on something that doesn't require baring your soul or revealing your innermost secrets. You might ask how they would handle a particularly challenging conversation or get their take on a cryptic memo from top management. You could follow that up by bouncing an idea off them to see how they think about things.

When it comes to peer coaches, you're looking for a handful of people, so you can afford to be choosy. They need to be people who give good, impartial advice and will keep your conversations confidential. If you sense they have their own agenda rather than your best interests at heart, then they're not a good candidate.

• Connectors

Part of the benefit of having a community of support is gaining access to opportunities that you wouldn't know about on your own. The world is becoming increasingly interconnected. But you don't have time to get to know everyone, nor do you need to know everyone. However, when you *are* looking for opportunities, it's useful to be able to activate your community to connect you with the right people. Whether you're trying to find a job, get introduced to a client prospect, hire a new team member, or uncover information that's not readily available, your network of connections is a rich source.

The thing is, the people who can lead you to opportunities won't always be directly in your community. This is where the "six degrees of separation" concept comes in. Initially proposed by Hungarian author Frigyes Karinthy (and validated by psychologist Stanley Milgram and others), the idea is to get to the edges of your network—your "weak ties"—to tap into broader networks where you can access fresh connections and opportunities.[22]

One of the easiest ways to extend your reach into a broader network of relationships is to get warm introductions from someone you already know. The people in your network who are especially good at this are connectors—those wonderful people who sit at the intersection of several other networks. Not only are they well-connected with people beyond those you already know, but they also delight in connecting people. If you're busy or shy, having one or two connectors in your community of support will be invaluable. One call to a connector can lead you to the precise person or opportunity you're looking for, without the endless legwork.

If you're thinking you don't know any connectors, think again. A connector, who may not be especially senior, may be hiding in plain sight. Take, for instance, the time we up-and-comers were discussing how we hoped to get Bob, the head of the Firm's biggest division, for our speaker series for new hires. He was notoriously hard to reach and certainly wouldn't have heard of any of us.

Just as we were about to resort to sending a cold email, Pam piped up, "I can call Bob for you." We turned to Pam in surprise. We knew her as the administrative support person who helped us with new hire onboarding and hadn't considered that she might know senior executives in lofty positions. But Pam had run the new associates training program for 25 years. She knew all the senior executives from when they were "wet behind the ears," including Bob, and was more than happy to connect us. Bob agreed to do the talk, and we realized the connector we needed was under our noses the entire time.

• Raving Fans

These are people who think you are wonderful and speak well of you whenever they can. They might be people you've mentored, team members you've led, colleagues you've collaborated with, or clients you've delivered results for. What they have in common is an appreciation for who you are and what you've done, a belief in your potential to do more, and the willingness to support you whenever they can.

Raving fans are useful on a personal level because they can remind you of all the great things you've done. When you're down or feeling sorry for yourself, they can lift your spirits and remind you of what you're like at your best. On a professional level, they're not shy to trumpet your success when you've had important accomplishments and advocate for you behind closed doors, where important decisions are discussed and made.

Whether they're internal or external to your organization and whatever their seniority levels, your raving fans appreciate what you've done for and with them and are supportive.

For example, a consulting client recommended me as an executive coach to the COO of the company where he was a board member. I later heard from the COO that he referred to me as "the best coach in the world."

For you, it may be a former boss who sits on the promotion committee who sings your praises when your name comes up, or a well-connected relative who's eager to recommend you to those in her business circles.

As you make a list of people who are likely to be your raving fans, look back at the decision-makers and influencers from your stakeholder map in Chapter 2 and see whether any of them make the list. If not, you'll want to convert them. Your sponsor is likely to be a raving fan as well; otherwise, they wouldn't risk their reputation to sponsor you for bigger and better opportunities.

Putting Building Your Community into Practice

When it comes to building your community of supporters, success requires both strategic assessment and intentional engagement. Most of us don't rigorously think about our networks. People are just there, scattered across our work relationships,

LinkedIn connections, and personal contacts. But if you want to accelerate your career progress while making the journey more enjoyable, it's worth being strategic about your community building.

Step 1: Assess your current community.

If you've already taken inventory of your existing relationships through the lens of the five key roles discussed, you're on your way. If not, now's the time to start. Whether mentally or on paper, create a simple list with your contacts' names and the roles they play—Sponsor, Mentor, Peer Coach, Connector, Raving Fan. You'll likely discover some pleasant surprises. Hidden gems who could provide precisely the support you need, as well as some obvious gaps that have been limiting your progress.

As you continue to map out your relationships, look for three things...

First, how diverse is your network? If 90% of your connections work in your organization or industry, you're limiting your access to fresh perspectives and opportunities. The most valuable networks include people with different backgrounds who can offer new viewpoints and connections. For example, if you're in cloud storage technology, knowing people in venture capital, cybersecurity, AI development, and enterprise sales could all be helpful down the road.

Second, what about the seniority levels in your network? While peer relationships are important, advancing in your career often requires connections with people who are at least two levels above where you are now. These relationships give you insight into higher-level thinking, access to opportunities that aren't posted on job boards, and credibility that can speed up your advancement.

Third, which of the five key roles are missing from your community? Maybe you have plenty of mentors, but no one who's actively advocating for your advancement behind closed doors. Or perhaps you have strong internal relationships but few external connectors who could introduce you to opportunities beyond your current organization.

Step 2: Build and maintain your strategic relationships.

Now that you know where you stand, the key is developing a sustainable approach to nurturing existing relationships while thoughtfully adding new ones.

• Start by saying yes, but more strategically.

Make it a habit to accept invitations that put you in contact with people who could become valuable members of your community—but be selective about which opportunities align with your goals and energy levels. This means prioritizing industry conferences where you can meet peers and potential mentors, alumni events that connect you with people in complementary fields, and professional association meetings relevant to your career aspirations.

Before committing, ask yourself: Will this event help me connect with the types of people I identified in my network assessment? Can I realistically show up as my best self, or am I already stretched too thin? If you're time-pressed, consider organizing group gatherings instead of accepting multiple one-on-one meetings. Not only is this more efficient, but it positions you as a valuable connector who helps others expand their networks as well. The key is being intentional about your networking investments rather than saying yes to everything that comes your way.

When you do commit to showing up, make it count. Arrive prepared with genuine curiosity about others and resist the urge to check your phone or mentally review your to-do list. The quality of your presence matters more than the quantity of events you attend. People remember how you made them feel, not how busy you appeared to be.

- **Develop a systematic approach to relationship maintenance.**

This is where many professionals fall short. They meet interesting people but fail to nurture those initial connections into meaningful relationships. The key is creating a system that works with your natural workflow rather than against it. Some people prefer digital tools like CRM systems, while others work better with simple spreadsheets, adding reminders on their calendar, or even handwritten notes.

Whatever system you choose, track three essential pieces of information: when you last connected, what you discussed, and when you should reach out again. The frequency depends on the relationship's importance and how well you know each other. Key supporters might warrant monthly contact, while broader network connections might only need quarterly or semi-annual check-ins. (More on this below.)

• **Focus on mutual value creation.**

The strongest professional relationships are built on reciprocity, but this doesn't mean keeping a transactional scorecard. Instead, look for ways to be genuinely helpful to others without expecting immediate returns. This might mean sharing relevant articles, making introductions between people in your network, or offering insights from your expertise. When you consistently add value to the professional lives of others, they naturally want to reciprocate when opportunities arise.

Building Professional Relationships Online

The fundamentals of relationship building haven't changed, but the ways to connect have expanded. Whether it's LinkedIn today or whatever platform emerges tomorrow, success comes from consistent, value-driven engagement rather than treating these tools like digital business cards.

The principles remain constant: share insights from your experience, engage thoughtfully with others' content, and personalize your outreach with specific references to their work or interests. When networking moves online—whether through dedicated platforms or remote events—the key is being more intentional about engagement and following up quickly to maintain momentum.

Creating Systems That Actually Work

Here's the thing about networking: the difference between people who get real value from their relationships and those who don't isn't about having the most contacts. It's about how they maintain those relationships over time. Without some kind of system, even your best connections will fade into distant memories.

1. Set up your relationship management system.

The best networkers treat relationship maintenance like any other important part of their job, with clear systems and consistent follow-through. Start by putting your contacts into different buckets based on their relevance to your current goals and how well you know them. As your career goals and situation change, make sure you reassess these categories.

Your Tier 1 contacts are the key players—sponsors, close collaborators, and your most important mentors. You'll want to connect with these people more often, say, monthly or quarterly, depending on the strength of the relationship.

Tier 2 includes important industry contacts, former colleagues in relevant positions, and potential mentors. Aim to touch base every three to six months.

Tier 3 is your broader professional network. Checking in once a year or engaging with their social media posts is probably enough.

For each person, keep track of the following:

- When you last talked and what you talked about.
- Any personal or professional details worth remembering for next time.
- When you should reach out again.

You don't need fancy software for this; a simple spreadsheet with columns for name, company, last contact date, notes, and next action works great. You might even jot it down in a notebook if that works best for you.

2. Stay in touch without being weird.

The best relationship maintenance doesn't feel forced or calculated. Build up a collection of genuine reasons to reconnect.

You might share articles they'd find interesting, introduce them to someone who could help them, congratulate them on work wins, or check in during big industry events or personal milestones.

The most successful network builders are the people who share valuable information and make useful connections for others. When you read something that would interest a specific contact, send it along with a quick note about why you thought of them. When you meet someone who could help make a connection in your network, make the introduction. This positions you as someone who adds value, not just someone who reaches out when you need something. Note: When you make introductions, it's best to check with both parties first.

Here's what matters most: consistency beats frequency every time. It's better to connect with your key contacts every six months like clockwork than to have bursts of networking activity followed by months of radio silence. People notice when you're reliable about staying in touch, even if the individual conversations are brief.

Converting Contacts to Raving Fans

Meeting people is easy. Turning those connections into raving fans who enthusiastically support your success is an art form that requires intention, patience, and strategic thinking.

Raving fans differ from regular network contacts because they don't just respect your work; they actively promote you and your accomplishments to others.

Understanding The Raving Fan Mindset

Raving fans are created when they respect your competence, like you as a person, and see mutual benefit in your success. A raving fan isn't just someone who can help you; they're someone who wants to help you and will do so even when you're not around.

Here's a good illustration: Tamara was one of many analysts in our department during my banking career. During our time working together, Tamara showed a genuine interest in my work and leadership approach. She asked thoughtful questions, implemented my suggestions, and occasionally shared relevant insights.

When I bumped into her several years later, she had moved to another firm, and I had switched careers entirely to start my coaching and speaking business. When she learned about my new direction, something remarkable happened. Without any prompting from me, Tamara immediately suggested she could introduce me to her Managing Director and recommend me as a speaker for their next corporate offsite.

Grateful for the introduction, I ended up conducting several workshops for her company, and they hired me to coach some of their executives. That single recommendation essentially launched my speaking and coaching business.

When she moved firms a few years later, Tamara hired me as her executive coach to help her advance to Managing Director (which she achieved in record time). Today, she would be top of mind for me to recommend for any number of roles. Through this mutually beneficial relationship, we have become each other's raving fans.

Creating a Foundation of Mutual Trust and Respect

The most effective raving fan relationships develop organically through a natural progression of deepening trust and mutual investment. It begins with establishing credibility through consistent excellence and reliability. People need to respect your competence before they'll advocate for you. This means delivering on commitments, demonstrating sound judgment, and showing genuine engagement with your work.

As credibility builds, successful relationship-builders focus on creating authentic connections. This happens through showing genuine interest in others' expertise and challenges, asking thoughtful questions, and finding ways to add value from your unique perspective. The key is making interactions feel valuable to the other person, not simply beneficial to you.

Over time, these consistent positive interactions create a foundation of mutual respect that can survive career transitions and changing circumstances. When opportunities arise to support each other's success, both parties are naturally inclined to help because the relationship feels genuinely beneficial rather than transactional.

The most powerful raving fan relationships are those where both people actively look for ways to support the other's advancement. This creates a self-reinforcing cycle where each success strengthens the relationship and increases both parties' willingness to advocate for each other.

The Long-Term Payoff

When done right, raving fan relationships become self-reinforcing assets that create value far beyond any individual transaction. Raving fans don't just help you once—they become ongoing advocates who think of you when opportunities arise, introduce you to their networks, and lend their credibility to your initiatives.

Note that raving fans can evolve into other types of relationships in your community of support. They may become mentors, connectors, or even sponsors, depending on their position and your career trajectory. Some of your strongest professional relationships will include elements of multiple categories from your network. That's why the investment in converting contacts to raving fans pays dividends throughout your career.

You're not just building a network—you're building a community of people who are genuinely invested in your success and excited to support your advancement when opportunities arise. And your ability to succeed with greater ease and speed is directly related to the breadth, depth, and quality of the community you build.

PERSONAL ACTION PLAN

1. Looking at the five key roles (Sponsor, Mentor, Peer Coach, Connector, Raving Fan), where are the biggest gaps in your current community of support? Consider: Who advocates for you behind closed doors? Who gives you trusted advice? Who connects you to new opportunities? Who enthusiastically promotes your work?

2. Reviewing your stakeholder map from Chapter 2, which key stakeholders could you work to convert into raving fans? Think about: Who already respects your work? Who have you helped succeed? Which relationships have mutual benefit potential? What would it take to deepen these connections?

3. Who are 1-2 specific people you want to add to your community over the next 3-6 months, and what value can you create for each other? Consider: What roles do you need filled? How can you be genuinely helpful to them? What's your approach for building these relationships?

4. What's your system for maintaining relationships with your community? Think about: How will you track important details? How often will you reach out to different tiers of contacts? What are your go-to ways of adding value (sharing articles, making introductions, celebrating their wins)?

5. **Which person in your current community could you reach out to this month to accelerate your career, and what specific help would you ask for?** Consider: Who has insights into opportunities you're pursuing? Who could make valuable introductions? Who could provide advice on your next career move?

6. **What's one specific action you'll take this week to strengthen your community of support?** Choose something concrete: Reach out to a former colleague, attend a networking event, or add value to someone in your network.

CONCLUSION

Tamara—the co-worker from Chapter 10 who would become my raving fan, and I hers—was right in the middle of the most challenging phase of her career. Things were changing without her realizing it. The formula that had helped her reach her current level of success was no longer working. In fact, working harder at the old plan was keeping her firmly stuck where she was. It was also exhausting.

Understanding this was a relief. No wonder things felt so hard. No wonder she felt like she needed a nine-month sabbatical to catch her breath. She also knew where she wanted to go; she wanted to earn a spot in the C-suite one day. She had taken all the right steps so far: she had gotten good grades in school, landed a job at a prestigious company, and outworked everyone else to stand out as the "go-to" person in the department.

In other words, she'd aced the initial part of her career. But now she felt like she was topping out. Those early promotions came quickly and easily, but she hadn't had a move up in almost three years, and she was getting worried. *Was she at risk of being one of those people who made a fast start only to flame out?*

She knew she could operate at a higher level, but sensed that her approach of outworking everyone else and being the consummate team player was no longer going to be enough. She felt like she was being taken for granted. Her accomplishments that management had once seen as miraculous were now getting her perfunctory pats on the head. She was working too hard to be accused of coasting, but her career trajectory was clearly slowing. Could her previously fast rise have been a fluke? She was still the same strong performer from three years ago ... maybe that was part of the problem.

The Shift that Changes Everything

What so many high achievers miss (Tamara included) is the fundamental shift that happens in every successful career: excellence in your current role is no longer enough. Decision-makers promote based on potential. Your potential to succeed at the next level must be easily visible to be on their radar.

As we went through the three key areas for career success—how to work with people, on the business, and on your self), Tamara started to see what she needed to do to move forward and regain her career momentum.

She recognized that her biggest opportunities for improvement were in the "self" category. She had been so nose-to-the-grindstone that she lost awareness of how her behaviors and approach to the job made her appear more junior than she was. For example, carrying a stack of papers as she scurried down the hall to the next meeting made her look like a disorganized assistant, and her natural tendency to listen and learn was keeping her from speaking up in meetings.

Alongside self-awareness, she needed to develop her executive presence. This had come up in several performance reviews, but since she didn't know exactly what to do to improve, she reverted to doing what she did best: grinding out excellent work. (Notice how the word "grind" comes up repeatedly.)

With her lack of executive presence, it may have been a blessing that she didn't yet have a high profile. However, she knew she would have to raise her profile with senior management if she hoped to join their ranks one day.

Another area in need of improvement was being strategic about the business. Staying focused on the here and now came at the expense of recognizing the future risks and opportunities for her business area. If she could spend even a fraction of her time zooming out to think about the trends and themes shaping the business, she felt sure she could become a strategic thinker. She couldn't think of one executive who was focused on the tactical—not even the head of operations. Even her boss invested time in strategic thinking and had ideas on what changes they needed to make to stay ahead of the competition.

Thankfully, Tamara also realized she had plenty of strengths to leverage to effect the necessary changes in these areas. She excelled at working with people. She kept her boss in the loop, communicated with colleagues in cross-divisional working groups, and led her team of product specialists. Her immediate circle of stakeholders liked and respected her, and her juniors spoke highly of her.

Tamara just needed to expand that circle to include decision-makers like the global product heads and executive committee members, as well as the various chiefs of staff and senior managers who influenced them. She also had good judgment and made sound decisions. She just needed to apply that skill beyond the execution of the projects that her team and she were tasked with.

When Tamara applied the framework to assess where she stood on the three key areas—People, Business, and Self—she saw what she needed to work on. You can too.

Your Third Way Forward

Let's return to our mission: to help you advance in your career without playing politics, selling your soul, or burning out.

If you've read this far, there's no doubt in my mind that you're too good a person and bring too much value to fall into the either-or trap: either sell out to play the game or grind harder just to find yourself falling further and further behind. You don't have to give in or give up.

This isn't about working harder or compromising your integrity to "play the game." There's a third path: strategically developing the skills that demonstrate your potential to key stakeholders while remaining authentic to your values and strengths. It's taking ownership of how you're perceived, not just what you produce.

Now that you know how to find that third way, you can advance in your career *and* feel great about yourself. No more struggling alone, unsure about what to do, or how to advocate for yourself with integrity.

By applying the lessons you've learned in the pages of this book and by developing the skills that demonstrate potential, you clear the path forward and position yourself to enjoy the career success you richly deserve.

Take Ownership Now

You're now the owner of your career trajectory. Along that path is that pivotal mid-career phase, where you must recognize and develop the skills needed to ensure your potential is visible...

At some point in your career, you will be focusing on how you work with people—whether managing your relationship with those all-important stakeholders, leading your team, or communicating in a way that influences outcomes. Other times, it will be working on the business—moving beyond the technical skills to become someone who creates more opportunities or growing your strategic vision and decision-making abilities. Often, it will be working on your *self* so you're more self-aware, able to build your presence and profile, or enhance your network of supporters.

Whether you use the assessment as a diagnostic or think it through on your own, take a moment to figure out: What is it you need to work on now? Why is that the most important skill to develop? What will developing it "buy" you?

Once you know what and why, it's all about *how* you choose to implement. First and foremost, it's about taking action, even if it's imperfect action. Don't let the fear of getting it wrong stop you from taking steps. Every time you act, you learn, which makes it an opportunity to refine your next move further.

It's about adapting the strategies and action steps in this book to your situation. Make the approach your own by aligning it with your skill set and values on the one hand, and the role and organization you're in on the other.

For example, if you're a strong communicator with great interpersonal skills and you value fairness, then this can show up in the way you eloquently stand up for those who aren't represented in the meeting. And while being direct in confronting a colleague might be the norm on a trading floor, the same approach might seem too aggressive in a nonprofit.

Since there's nuance in how people will react, you'll need feedback along the way so you can adjust your approach and recalibrate. This is where it helps to have mentors, trusted peers, or an executive coach to help you navigate and make midcourse adjustments. Any time you're making a change, it's best when paired with thinking partners.

Navigating the ups and downs of your career successfully isn't a paint-by-numbers exercise. There's a degree of improvising and customizing based on how things unfold.

So, develop the habit of regularly paying attention to your career and reassessing the skills you can leverage and the ones you need to work on next.

Your Next Bold Move

You now know what to do next: you're clear on the one or two skills to focus on, and you're taking ownership of your career. That means you have the confidence to carve your own path, because clarity breeds confidence. And you have the courage to take action because you can see how doable it all is.

You're on the way to finding your own approach to career success, armed with a framework and actionable steps for navigating the shifting demands of career advancement.

As you move forward, here are a few practical strategies for making your next moves and freeing yourself up to have the career you've dreamed of:

- **Take action rather than overthink it.** You'll learn more from imperfect action than from staying stuck trying to get it perfect. If there's one thing I've learned, it's that acts of omission are more often the cause of regret than acts of commission. So, stop negotiating with yourself.

- **Do experiments.** An experiment is the smallest possible step you can take and still get the information you need to determine whether you're on the right track. It's okay to take baby steps. You don't need to make big sweeping changes. Focus on the small hinges that swing open big doors.

- **Don't go it alone.** Form a small team of trusted peers, tap into wise mentors, get feedback from people you trust and respect, work with a coach, join a mastermind, or tap into resources for career-minded people like my Career Mastery membership.

- **Trust your instincts.** When you permit yourself to look deep inside, you know what's best for you. Your career will go fastest and strongest when it feels authentic to you. Just make sure you understand the difference between the natural resistance that comes from stepping outside your comfort zone versus the warning signals from doing something that runs counter to your core values.

- **Reframe when you feel resistance.** When you're holding yourself back from doing something you know you want to do, and it's important for your future aspirations, reframing the action into something energizing will help you overcome that resistance.

- **Feel the fear and do it anyway.** Sometimes, it all comes down to this: pushing through the fear. Break yourself out of your habitual behaviors, or you'll remain right where you are—or even fall behind. And that's scarier still.

- **Be kind to yourself.** Change takes time. As one of my mentors says, "You can't rush sourdough bread. It's going to take the time it takes." Be patient and encouraging. And just keep going.

The path I've outlined isn't just about career advancement; it's about finding greater satisfaction and purpose in your work. When you demonstrate your potential in the three key areas, you position yourself for promotion and create a more fulfilling professional experience along the way.

You have everything you need: clarity on what matters most, confidence in your ability to develop the skills, and the courage to take that first bold step toward your future potential.

When you own your potential, you own your career future. And the world needs good people like you in positions of greater influence and impact.

The only question that remains is, what will you do first?

ENDNOTES

Chapter 1

1. 2024 Work Trend Index Annual Report, "AI at Work is Here. Now Comes the Hard Part," Microsoft and LinkedIn, May 8, 2024, https://www.microsoft.com/en-us/worklab/work-trend-index/ai-at-work-is-here-now-comes-the-hard-part.

2. State of the Global Workplace: 2023 Report, "The Voice of the World's Employees," Gallup, accessed July 13, 2025, https://www.gallup.com/workplace/349484/state-of-the-global-workplace.aspx.

Chapter 3

3. Amy C. Edmondson, *The Fearless Organization: Creating Psychological Safety in the Workplace for Learning, Innovation, and Growth* (Hoboken, NJ: John Wiley & Sons, 2018), https://www.hbs.edu/faculty/Pages/item.aspx?num=54851.

4. Morgan McCall, Michael Lombardo, and Robert A. Eichinger. "The 70-20-20 Rule for Leadership Development." *Center for Creative Leadership*, April 24, 2025. https://www.ccl.org/articles/leading-effectively-articles/70-20-10-rule.

5. Shirzad Chamine, *Positive Intelligence: Why Only 20% of Teams and Individuals Achieve Their True Potential and How You Can Achieve Yours* (Austin: Greenleaf Book Group Press, 2012).

Chapter 4

6. Judith Glaser, *Conversational Intelligence* (New York: Routledge, 2016).

7. J. Luo and R. Yu, "Follow the Heart or the Head? The Interactive Influence Model of Emotion and Cognition," Frontiers in Psychology 6, no. 573 (2015), https://doi.org/10.3389/fpsyg.2015.00573.

Chapter 5

8. Timothy Ferriss, *The 4-Hour Workweek: Escape 9-5, Live Anywhere, and Join the New Rich* (New York: Harmony, 2009).

Chapter 6

9. "Colin Powell's 40-70 Rule." 42 Courses: Entertain Your Brain. Accessed June 20, 2025. https://www.42courses.com/blog/home/2019/12/10/colin-powells-40-70-rule.

10. Barry Schwartz, *The Paradox of Choice: Why More Is Less* (New York: HarperCollins, 2004).

11. Brian Tracy, *Eat That Frog: 21 Great Ways to Stop Procrastinating and Get More Done in Less Time* (San Francisco: Berrett-Koehler Publishers, 2017).

12. Martin, Roger. *The Opposable Mind: How Successful Leaders Win Through Integrated Thinking.* Harvard Business Review Press, 2007.

13. Haden, Jeff. "Amazon Founder Jeff Bezos: This is How Successful People Make Such Smart Decisions." *Inc.*, December 3, 2018. https://www.inc.com/jeff-haden/amazon-founder-jeff-bezos-this-is-how-successful-people-make-such-smart-decisions.html.

Chapter 7

14. Judith Glaser, *Conversational Intelligence* (New York: Routledge, 2016).

Chapter 8

15. Carol S. Dweck, *Mindset: The New Psychology of Success* (New York: Random House, 2006).

16. Kolbe-A™ Index, Kolbe Corp, accessed June 21, 2025, https://www.kolbe.com/kolbe-a-index.

17. Simon Alexander Ong, *Energize* (Penguin Business, 2022).

18. Jim Loehr and Tony Schwartz, "Manage Your Energy, Not Your Time," *Harvard Business Review*, October 1, 2007, https://hbr.org/2007/10/manage-your-energy-not-your-time.

19. James Clear, *Atomic Habits: An Easy & Proven Way to Build Good Habits & Break Bad Ones.* (New York: Avery, 2018), https://jamesclear.com/atomic-habits.

20. Joseph Luft and Harry Ingham. "The Johari Window: A Graphic Model of Interpersonal Awareness." In *Proceedings of the Western Training Laboratory in Group Development*, Los Angeles: University of California, Los Angeles, 1955.

Chapter 9

21. Liro Jääskeläinen, Vasily Klucharev, Ksenia Panidi, and Anna N. Shestakova, "Neural Processing of Narratives: From Individual Processing to Viral Propagation," *Frontiers* 14, no. 253 (2020): https://doi.org/10.3389/fnhum.2020.00253.

Chapter 10

22. Paul Kirvan, "Six Degrees of Separation," *TechTarget, July 18, 2022. https://www.techtarget.com/whatis/definition/six-degrees-of-separation.*

ACKNOWLEDGMENTS

This book exists because of the many people who have supported, challenged, and inspired me along the way.

At the top of the list of people to thank is my amazing book coach and publisher, Ann Sheybani. Without her deep expertise, sage guidance, and keen eye for what makes a book readable and relatable, *Visible* would not be what it is today. Thanks for encouraging me, correcting my mistakes, extracting the nuggets, shaping my manuscript, tightening up my message, and telling me when to stop endlessly iterating! And thank you to Walt and the entire Summit Press team for believing in my work and turning my "book project" into a reality.

Thank you to my team—especially Mickey and Renee—for holding down the fort in the business while I wrote (and rewrote), and to Mickey, Renee, Natalie, Clarice, and Lynsi for providing input on the myriad decisions and supporting items that go into creating a book, making it possible for me to add value to our clients and audience far beyond what I could do on my own.

To my family, who've given me the freedom to work on my mission and inspired me to keep going. Thank you, Len,

Kristen, Renee, and Natalie, for your understanding, support, and willingness to talk through my latest ideas on leadership and career advancement.

To my parents, Shu and K.C., who are tremendous role models for what it means to be a good person and a good leader. I've learned so much from you. Thank you for the lifetime of knowledge, experience, and wisdom I draw on to help others.

I'm thankful for my dear friends, colleagues, sponsors, and mentors throughout my career, especially at Morgan Stanley. You know who you are, and I am grateful beyond words for your support and the opportunity to learn from you about leadership, being a "rainmaker," and what it takes to have a successful career in a fast-paced, rapidly changing, and competitive world while still being yourself.

And a special thanks to my clients, workshop participants, Career Mastery members, and the broader community of good people who have followed my work. I am grateful that you've trusted me with your challenges and opportunities and given me insight into the strategies that are working for you. Thank you for allowing me to walk beside you on your career journey—I can't wait to see what's next for you!

ABOUT THE AUTHOR

MAY BUSCH works with good people who want to advance their careers and make the difference they're meant to make in the world—without sacrificing their values in the process.

After her own 24-year rise to chief operating officer of Morgan Stanley Europe, she discovered the hidden shift that separates those who advance from those who plateau: it's not enough to deliver excellent performance; you also need to make your potential visible to key decision-makers.

As founder of Career Mastery™, May has developed a practical framework built around three strategic pillars—working with *people*, working on the *business*, and working on your *self*. Her approach has guided thousands of professionals toward promotions, leadership roles, and greater career satisfaction.

A Harvard College and Harvard Business School graduate, May serves as senior advisor for leadership at Arizona State University. She also provides executive coaching to senior leaders around the world. Her work proves that good people can finish first, creating positive change that ripples through organizations and industries.

Everything May shares is what she wishes she had during her own journey. She brings the same insight, integrity, and practical wisdom to her work that she brings to her roles as mother, mentor, and advocate for authentic leadership.

Now it's time to take action on the insights you've gained and advance your career on your own terms. You can do this! And the resources I mentioned throughout the book will make it easier.

Go to **www.thevisiblebook.com/resources** to access free tools, templates, and other valuable stuff.

This is your time to go for it, and I am rooting for your success!

www.ingramcontent.com/pod-product-compliance
Lightning Source LLC
Chambersburg PA
CBHW060410130626
46555CB00005B/2021